BHM

Love your Hat

MW01254664

OWN YOUR POWER

OWN YOUR
POWER

NO EXCUSES. NO BULLSH*T. YOUR TIME IS NOW.

JAYSON WALLER | CEO POWERHOME SOLAR

LIONCREST
PUBLISHING

OWN YOUR POWER
No Excuses. No Bullsh*t. Your Time is Now.

ISBN   978-1-5445-2387-3   *Hardcover*

978-1-5445-2385-9   *Paperback*

978-1-5445-2386-6   *Ebook*

978-1-5445-2388-0   *Audiobook*

CONTENTS

INTRODUCTION

BUSINESS, BS, AND BEGINNING

To get where you want to be, you simply must begin.

Being successful in business—and in life, love, and everything else—begins at some point. That specific point is up to you. You make the decision when to begin your most successful journey. It starts when you stop believing your own bullshit.

Think about it.

> **Every great entrepreneurial journey or massively successful business has a story behind it that includes an underdog and a pivotal moment that changes everything.**

It's not a cliché. Success demands that the underdog changes the course of their story and that starts with switching up your underdog story.

The truth is that everyone thinks they're an underdog in some way. And they are. Every person has stuff they hate about their past, their present, and themselves—crappy attributes, qualities, and circumstances they think are holding them back from what they want.

You included.

You wouldn't have picked up a book called *Own Your Power* if you didn't think you were an underdog on some level.

We spend so much time believing the BS and seeing ourselves as the underdog that success feels out of reach—like success is a chapter in someone else's story.

Being an underdog doesn't mean you have to be broke.

Or that you grew up in a family with drug problems or dysfunctional parents.

Or that you have some physical handicap.

Your underdog story could be that you were a kid who didn't have to earn anything and was pampered for your entire existence, so you have no real-life skills. Or maybe you had a family tragedy and haven't been able to recover. Maybe you struggle with anxiety or some other kind of "deficiency."

Perhaps you've been slaving away at your business and feel like everyone else is hitting success while you tread water.

> **The underdog mentality is *any* BS story you tell yourself as justification for why you don't have what you want.**

Everyone has demons they fight. I have my problems. You have yours. But here's the truth about all our stories: the BS ideas we tell ourselves are what hold us back from that pivotal moment that puts us on our success journey.

It's time to disrupt those thoughts.

It's time to begin.

STARTING WITH THE RIGHT STORY

Here's the big not-so-secret secret: being an underdog is not about your circumstances, bad luck, poor timing, or whatever other excuse a human brain can come up with to justify why you're not where you want to be. What's in the way of you is you. It's your own head trash.

I know this from personal experience. I grew up in a baby-blue trailer with a rusted underbelly, but today I am the founder and CEO of POWERHOME, a solar panel company that has done over $1 billion in sales.

So, dudes, ladies, everyone: I'm talking to you. You can live the life you dream about, despite perhaps a crappy start to life, a dead-end job, the size of your bank account, or your gender, race, or whatever. Fill in the blank with what you think is wrong with you. It's basically all the same. And none of it makes a good excuse.

Maybe you're playing small because you're married and have kids to feed, and you're afraid to look into their doe-eyed faces and say you've failed them. So you suffer through days at a soul-crushing job—or two, like my dad did—while you dream of starting your own business, getting ahead at your company, or taking a leap of faith into the passion project you've been dreaming about.

Or maybe you don't have anyone around you who has accomplished what you want to achieve. Maybe you have people around you who are limited. It's also possible you are more successful than you ever thought you would be today, but your past still holds you back from going bigger and succeeding greater. Do you accept a moderately good life and secretly think, *Is this it?*

Let's get real—is that how you want to live your life?

If it is, that's cool. My point is: whatever you're doing, it had better damn well empower you.

Your underdog story should also empower you. You must start

thinking differently about who you are, where you've been and how you'll go higher—your own version of success.

Before you can begin, you must get your story straight, and that starts with owning your power.

BEGINNING: STEP ONE

If you're scared of what it might mean to own your power, I get you. I've been there too. I'm not saying it's not real. But it's only in your head. You can beat fear. Don't wimp out. If I get my way, now that I have you reading this book, you won't. You have what it takes.

Most people are lions who live like sheep. They follow along and go with the flow while desperately wanting to lead. They have genius ideas, but they hold back from sharing them with the world. They don't play to win—they play to avoid losing. I know what that looks like.

My parents were blue-collar survivors. My dad worked his ass off as a laborer at a Corning plant that made fiber for companies like AT&T. My mom decorated cakes at a grocery store. Between their jobs, we had milk in the fridge, though there were times when it was not much and other times when the milk was gone with only a half jar of pickles and a shelf of condiments. I'm not knocking either of my parents. We got by. But it was a rough start to my story.

I was the kid who wore the off-brand Tommy Hilfigers and got bullied at school. Kids can be mean.

"That's not a real Tommy," they'd say.

"You live in that trailer park, don't you?" was another common tease I heard from my peers. "Nice car, you loser," they'd say.

Eventually, I dropped out of school. And I got my girlfriend pregnant at eighteen.

I was the underdog from the baby-blue trailer with a rusted underbelly. Your underdog story might be similar. Or maybe you had it worse than me. Or maybe you're just thinking, *Geez, I thought I had it bad,* and now you're wondering if you're not successful because you didn't have it bad enough! You see what our brains make up? It's like I said: time to disrupt that BS.

Every great entrepreneurial journey or massively successful business has a story behind it that includes an underdog and a pivotal moment that changes everything.

The high-school dropout with the eighteen-year-old pregnant girlfriend had his pivotal moment—honestly, a few pivotal moments.

I went on to build two multimillion-dollar businesses and one billion-dollar business from zero while the haters mocked me. Now our solar panels are on NFL football stadium roofs, and I'm a household name, with my face in all our commercials.

Oh, and the girl I got pregnant? Her name is Liz. I married

her even though her family hated my guts. And we all get along today.

The baby? That's my daughter Hannah. She's smart and talented and beautiful inside and out. Now she has her own children. We got through it.

In 2019, I was one of the first guys without an MBA from Harvard or Princeton or any other preppy school to win the Ernst & Young Emerging Entrepreneur of the Year award. After they gave me the award, a room full of the world's top business minds with their MBAs and suits told me I had to tell my story. They said I should start a podcast or write a book.

I realized that wasn't just a good idea—it was my duty. Any underdog who wins has an obligation to tell their hero story in some way. They suggested two ways. So I did both.

Step One: Believe you can.

BEGINNING: STEP TWO

I now host a top-three Apple podcast called *True Underdog*, where I interview successful people who share their own underdog stories. I sit down regularly to talk to high-profile guests like Barry Sanders (ten-year running back for the NFL's Detroit Lions), David Meltzer (Co-Founder of Sports 1 Marketing, with $20 billion in relationship capital), and Peter Mallouk (President and Chief Investment Officer of Creative Planning, an advisory firm with $90 billion in assets.) Many of them are also now my good friends.

On the book front, at first it was funny for me to think about writing one. I think I've only ever read one book myself. I could barely spell entrepreneur! But as I talked to more people on my podcast—from insanely rocking businessmen like Chipotle CEO Monty Moran to big-name successes like Kevin O'Leary from *Shark Tank* and real estate investor Grant Cardone—and connected with my listeners, I knew this book had to be written.

The big questions from my underdog story that had to be answered: how did I crack the underdog code to become the alpha I was born (and we are all born) to be? And how did this lead to my success in business?

The simple answer: I believed I could and went after it. As for how I did it, it comes down to the principles I live and have laid out for you in this book.

When reality kicked the crap out of me, these principles helped me keep my head down and keep going.

No one showed me how. That would have been nice. Though, maybe not. Having done it all on my own is why I am so passionate about helping others do the same—it's addicting. That's why I wrote this book.

But listen, let's get one thing clear: I didn't write it to motivate you. I wrote it to inspire you. There's a big difference. Motivation is great, but it's short term. Inspiration has an active component. When you feel truly inspired, the emotion is enough to propel you into action.

Most importantly, when it comes to your mindset, you must run the show. You need to master your mindpower. And you must act. Grind it out.

Remember this: insights are great, but it's action that gets you to where you want to go.

In the next chapters, I'm going to share personal stories to show you how someone else overcame their shit. Use the stories in this book to start looking at your own story differently. I get deeply personal and deliver the raw facts—good and bad. I so badly want you to win in whatever way it looks like for you.

> **If you have no one in your corner saying you can, I'll be the first to say it now: *you can*.**

Belief is not enough. To transform your underdog story and pivot to massive success, you need practical tools. Remember, I'm just a trailer park kid. But I've also been a White House dinner guest. My past did not dictate my future.

I live by eight simple principles that have been massive to my business success. Namely, I live a life of *no excuses*. These eight principles taught me how to overcome my "trailer park mindset" and the barriers it created. By committing to these eight principles, I have the life that my underdog story never even thought was possible. Do you need to follow all eight principles? Perhaps, but feel free to flip to any chapter that speaks to where you are in your story right now.

EIGHT PRINCIPLES FOR A NO-EXCUSES LIFE

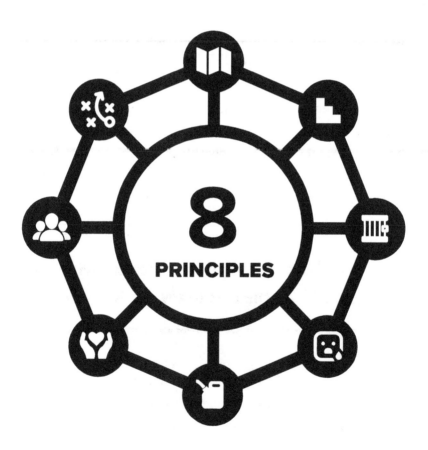

1. **Make Your Own Map:** Don't let other people's situations or ideas dictate your life. Develop your own fearless vision for what your story looks like and how success comes to you.

2. **There's No Elevator in Life—You've Gotta Take the Stairs:** You can't cheat your way to success. Cheating eventually leads to failure. Don't try to hack life because it never works out.

3. **Never Be Held Hostage:** You always have a choice. Own your circumstances and build systems so that you never feel forced to do what you don't want to do.

4. **Scared Money Don't Make Money:** Bet on yourself to get what you want. Getting what you want in any area of life requires taking risks. Swallow your fear and act.

5. **Turn Failure into Fuel:** Failure is part of success. Embrace it. Failure leads you closer to success because it makes you wiser and more resilient.

6. **Love Your Haters:** Success is the ultimate revenge. Live with more class, empathy, and an "everybody wins" attitude. Ignore the haters otherwise.

7. **Team Out:** All people can make you better. People are the most important building blocks to achieving great success in life.

8. **Focus on the Play-by-Play:** Stay the course and focus on small milestones only. Incremental progress trumps massive wins.

Reading this book and actively participating in what you learn might be your pivot point. It doesn't matter what shit you have been dealt in life or how bad it is—with the right skills, you can get where you want to be. Pivoting and succeeding requires training.

Each chapter has an **Own Your Power Challenge** to help you think about each concept, with steps to put you directly into action.

Draw a line in the sand now. There's no going back. And the good news is there's nothing complicated about what I'm about to lay out.

Step Two: Take action.

CHAPTER ONE

PRINCIPLE #1—MAKE YOUR OWN MAP

"How the fuck did I get here?"

If you have had any success, whether being promoted on the job or in your own business venture, I'm betting you've had a WTF moment of your own—that moment when the impossible becomes true in your underdog story.

The night I won the 2019 Ernst & Young Emerging Entrepreneur of the Year Award, I had a WTF moment.

It was long after midnight. Liz and I had been partying late with a bunch of famous businesspeople and millionaires. Now we were back at the Omni Hotel at The Battery Atlanta where we'd been put up in an executive suite with a balcony that looked onto the field where the Atlanta Braves play.

I turned out the lights, lay down, and thought, *Wow, that was a cool day.*

But I didn't fall asleep to that thought. Instead, my brain flashed back to where I came from. I was eighteen years old again, back at University Hospital staring at nine babies, not knowing which was mine. That was the day my daughter Hannah was born.

Two lives started the day my firstborn came into the world. One was hers. The other was my rebirth.

I didn't know it in that moment, but everything was about to change. I wanted to see my baby girl so bad, but I wasn't allowed.

"Excuse me. I'm here to see Elizabeth Stalvey," I said to the nurse.

I stood in front of the admissions nurse at the front counter of the birth unit at University Hospital, where I had rolled up with my buddy Ben.

She scanned her list. "There's no one here by that name," she said.

We were two eighteen-year-old kids pretending to be men. The fact that I needed a sidekick was an obvious tell. My First Union sales rep shirt didn't make me any more adult either. To the nurse, we were two little boys playing dress-up.

"Uh...yeah, there is," I said. "Liz is here now. She was induced. She's having our baby today. Her mom's and sister's cars are in the parking lot. I just saw them."

The nurse checked her list again. "No. There's no one here with that name. Sorry." She didn't really look sorry.

It turned out that Liz's mom made her use an alias at the hospital because she didn't want me there. I was a high school dropout, the trailer park kid who knocked up her seventeen-year-old daughter.

The entire pregnancy had been a fight between Liz's mother and me. Her mom tried to get us to abort Hannah or give her up for adoption. We fought Liz's mom hard and just long enough that abortion was no longer an option. She retaliated by admitting Liz to a maternity home, which is a residential facility where women go to have babies, and often so it's kept a secret.

I had to break Liz out of that place. One night a buddy and I drove up to the side of the building with the window to her dorm room. Moments later, a seven-month-pregnant Liz slid a panel of glass open and popped the screen out with a pair of tweezers. One step at a time, she descended two flights of a shaky fire escape. Then we put her in my car and drove away. So the fact we'd even made it to this day at the hospital was a damn miracle.

"Are you serious? I can't see my kid being born?" I said to the nurse.

The best she could do was direct us to the visitation area to see all the babies in the maternity ward. This was in 1998, so these were the days before protection laws. Anyone was allowed to view the latest batch of newly baked newborns through a glass window. We didn't know which baby was which, but we could go see them.

So we took the elevator up one level. I had a bulky Polaroid camera around my neck, which I wore like a rapper's neck bling. I was proud of it. I'd saved up for seven months to buy it so I could use it specifically for this day. I had imagined handing it to Ben and—click—having him capture the first moments of me holding my little girl.

The gadget was also a badge of progress—evidence I was doing okay in life. Sure, I'd dropped out of school, but I'd also landed a First Union sales job. I'd moved out of my parents' trailer. I had an apartment of my own. Once I was a dad, I figured I would get a lot of use out of my new Polaroid toy. Life would finally be good enough for taking pictures.

But standing there snapping photos of nine unknown newborns, I questioned my purchase for the first time. This camera was supposed to be for capturing the first photo of my baby—not a group shot of her and her eight new cooing buddies.

Later that night, Ben and I sat with my parents around their kitchen table. We searched the baby faces in the photos looking for traces of me. One by one, we tried to figure out which baby was mine.

That was one of the best days of my life. It was one of the worst too. I cried my ass off right there at my parents' kitchen table. No more trying to be a grown-ass man. I was a hot fucking mess. I snapped. But in the right kind of way because I also woke up.

I hit an emotional breaking point. I was sick of being denied what I wanted in life. The story I had been telling myself for years was that I could never get what I really wanted—I didn't qualify. Sitting at that kitchen table, that story finally got old. So I drew my own damn start line and walked across it.

Everything must change. I'm on a mission now. I can't fail. Game. On.

The shift I went through that day forever molded my approach to life, and it persists to this day. My mantra now is every day's a playoff game.

The one thing that hasn't changed is that I still only play to win. By the end of this book, if I have my way, you will start operating as if every day is a playoff game too. And better, you won't have to go through the kind of shit I did to start thinking this way.

Fast forward two decades. I'm married to Liz. We have four great kids. I'm a grandfather because Hannah has her own children now. But I still have flashbacks about that day. Maybe a little lingering PTSD at times. This is why when something amazing happened to me, like winning the 2019 Ernst & Young Emerging Entrepreneur of the Year Award, my brain screamed, *What the fuck? This can't be happening to me.*

In business, this happens a lot for any entrepreneur playing to win.

Take Kevin Plank, for example. You've probably worn his clothes. While playing college football, he had the spark for the idea called Under Armour. Starting a clothing company normally requires that you take on investors. Instead, Kevin saved $20,000 of his own money and went into $40,000 of credit card debt to get Under Armour off the ground in 1996. In the first year, he only made $17,000 in sales. Now that's a WTF moment. It's also the type of event that happens and causes entrepreneurs to change course and lose sight of where they are trying to go. Fear sets in. Doubt. The odds feel stacked against you. Kevin kept following his own map. Despite long odds, growing credit card interest, and a market that didn't yet understand the product, Kevin kept on track by contracting directly with twelve NFL teams and picking up new sales from there. He was consistent and persistent. Perseverance. In 2019, Under Armour hit $5 billion in sales and doesn't seem to be slowing down its massive growth anytime soon. The point is that he didn't follow anyone's map. He set his own course and was relentless in following it.

Owning your power starts with knowing where you want to go. You may not know how you're going to get there or how long it will take, but don't deviate from the destination.

The next time you put on a pair of Ray-Bans or get your reading glasses at LensCrafters, think about a poor kid with nine fingers who made it possible for you. This kid is Leonardo Del Vecchio. He was one of five kids born to his widowed mother. His mother put him in an orphanage, which had to have sucked. Then, when he got too old for the orphanage, he went to work in a factory making molds for auto parts and eyeglass frames and lost part of his finger on the job. Do you think the story on repeat in his head was very great at this point? No, but what I am positive is true is that he knew he was not going to die a nine-finger orphan who worked in a factory his entire life. At twenty-three, he opened his own molding shop. Today, he is the Founder and Chairman of Luxottica, which makes brands like Ray-Ban and Oakley, with 6,000 retail shops like Sunglass Hut and LensCrafters. His estimated net worth is now above $10 billion dollars. He made his own map.

Reciting your underdog story over and over again in your head while following the plans and expectations of other people is an act of insanity. If you are tired of not having the exact life you want and deserve, then you must change it by making your own map. I keep repeating this so it sticks in your head.

Underdog stories exist everywhere.

Take Mike Ashley, for example. He is the Founder of Sports Direct. He is a fellow high school dropout. At sixteen, he left school to play squash and he became nationally recognized. But then, without warning, an injury ended his career, and he was left out in the cold with no cash. I don't know the guy personally, but I am willing to bet that he had some tears at his own kitchen table. I'm also willing to bet that, like me, he woke up.

Everything must change. I'm on a mission now. I can't fail. Game. On.

Mike Ashley is now one of the most powerful people in British business, worth an estimated £6.6 billion. Ashley has reportedly made most of his fortune through buying sports brands. He owns Donnay, Karrimor and Kangol, to name a few. Most notable, perhaps, is Dunlop Slazenger, which he bought for £40 million. He definitely did not follow other people's map. How did he go from high school dropout and defunct athlete to billionaire? Those details are in his book.

I can give you hundreds of stories like these that prove my point. There is no one way to live your best life. So let's start by figuring out what story is keeping you from making a map and following it.

WHAT'S YOUR UNDERDOG STORY?

You may feel that you are an underdog, both personally and professionally. Perhaps you were bullied in school; perhaps you have a job where you are treated as a lowly underling; perhaps you own a business that is fighting for survival against the competition. My story began when I was a child and continued into early adulthood.

The beginnings of the **Make Your Own Map** principle took shape in the early days of my life, back before I even knew what to call it. Back when my own stories about my life ran the show.

We all have stories that we use to rationalize why we're the underdog. When life doesn't turn out the way you want, there's probably some crap story you use to rationalize it. When your business fails, you decide that it was because your employees didn't do their jobs, not because you might have had a faulty business plan, or sucked at sales or had weak management in place.

You're too old. Or too young. Or you didn't go to school. Or you don't have enough money to start that business. Or your front teeth are too crooked. Even people who seem to have it good have a story—maybe you were born privileged and have money but no life skills.

The circumstances don't matter. The story is what holds us back.

I know this now but didn't when I was a kid. My parents did their best, but we didn't have a lot of money growing up. I had a lot of, "Wow. What would that be like?" moments. Others always had what I didn't.

Even though I was a trailer park kid with knockoff clothes, it wasn't all bad. Every summer, my parents took me and my two siblings, Jeremy and Jessi, to Disneyland. It was the only trip we took each year. And they saved all their money for it. We lived in Phoenix, Arizona, until I was fourteen years old. Our family couldn't afford to fly to Disney, so we drove to California, usually in a car that didn't have air conditioning.

Most of the trip's budget was spent on the tickets that got us into the park. The rest of the dollars my parents had saved were carefully rationed to make them last. Each penny was allocated for basic survival expenses to make the trip happen. There was the cost of gas to get us between the colored gates of the park and our shoddy motel room (not a hotel—there's a difference) with wall-to-wall wood paneling and pilled floral bedding that you didn't really want to sleep in.

The one-star experience that supported our time at the park didn't stop us. The whole family loved our Disney trips.

We'd go early and stand in horribly long lines with ear-to-ear grins plastered to our faces. We'd alternate screaming and laughing on all the rides. We were like the idyllic, way-too-happy families from the Disneyland commercials, all hands in the air on the roller coasters, lots of Mickey Mouse high-fives, and wide-eyed happiness in all the theme park madness. Is it truly "the happiest place on earth"? I certainly thought so.

Each afternoon, we put the fun on pause to hike back to the motel. My mom made peanut butter and strawberry jelly or bologna and mustard sandwiches, with all the house-brand ingredients tucked into a Dempster cooler. We'd chow them down, slurp back our one rationed can of soda each, and then head back.

Somewhere between the minivan and the line for rides, I could see a future where I was in control. Where I could buy the snacks at the park if I wanted to and stay in an actual hotel. I started to see life as a map with places I knew I wanted to avoid and other places I wanted to travel to.

Eventually, I realized I was the driver of the car following the map too. And over time, I got tired of driving the rutted roads—or worse, being driven by someone else down dusty routes. I wanted control. You can only take shit for so long. The day Hannah arrived was a departure point for me. It was my turn to drive.

You can live life like every day is a playoff game, no matter who you are or where you came from. You don't have to have an unplanned kid or a trailer park existence or a one-star Disneyland childhood.

You make your own map in life, and you can start any time.

A MAP FOR YOUR LIFE; A PLAN FOR YOUR BUSINESS

Every day that you wake up is a new day to navigate life. You're in the driver's seat, figuring out what route to take moment to moment. Take the scenic route? Or the highway? Or maybe you drive right through the city core in a bright-blue Lamborghini because you're a loud asshole like someone I know who likes to make his presence known. Bam! Go for it. That's cool too.

This "every day is a new day" type of thinking applies to your business as well. Do you want to explore a new marketing campaign? Expand your product offerings? Increase the size of your business? You're at the wheel; make the most of it. What can you do today?

Your journey is your own. The business you create is your own. You get to pick it. You get to design it. You get to make the business plan. Nobody else. It's your God-given right.

Whether or not you realize it, you're also headed toward a

destination. And again, you can decide what that is. You can create and redesign your business plans as many times as you need to.

We often forget that we have this power. For the first quarter of my life, I lived like I didn't have a choice. Think about it: have you ever driven and barely noticed the road? Or driven on cruise control with a GPS babbling at you, where you wait for the voice to tell you where to go: "Take the next right on Jamieson Avenue." Sure, it makes driving easier. But what are you going to do when you lose your Wi-Fi connection?

Too many people live their lives and run their businesses this way, just following the route someone else is dictating.

Honestly, some people aren't even driving the car they've been given! They just stay put with their metaphorical keys in the ignition, never taking any steps forward. That will never make you happy or successful. I'd go as far as to say it is not a life at all.

You'll never get back the time you waste on the wrong street following the wrong map. That means every decision in life has value—but that doesn't mean we should be paralyzed by those decisions. Every action you take results in useful feedback, even if it involves a business mistake or failure. You learn what to do next. The only real way to fail is not to choose a path.

If you turn right and don't like that path, you can make a U-turn. Congratulations! You win. Or maybe you'll find a hidden route to get there faster. Congratulations! You win. You redesign your marketing strategy. Maybe it turns out the turn was the best decision you ever made, or maybe it felt like the worst, and it'll take some time to recover. Congratulations! You win.

When my family can't decide or my teams flip-flop and stall, it drives me crazy. Either we do or we don't, and if we decide to get there, it's a win no matter what. The catch is that you must be tuned into life all the time. If you're the driver, the mapmaker, and the navigator—or the driving force behind your business—you must pay attention. You must notice the path you're on, think about where you've been, and remind yourself where you're going.

Every single choice we make creates our maps or drives the success or failure of our companies and moves us closer to the destinations we're driving toward. Every day I make my map, just like you do, in all my choices from moment to moment. Am I going to go to the gym today? Or maybe I'll decide to tell POWER-HOME SOLAR I quit (ha!). Am I going to drive my son to school today or send him on the bus?

We get one life. We don't get a do-over or a reset, so we must be strategic. **Make Your Own Map** is a principle that operates in life as well as business. It helps you keep focused on where you want to go instead of just driving to drive. I can easily spot the difference between someone who has a map and someone who doesn't. It is also evident in businesses that flounder and ultimately fail. You need a map or a business plan to keep you on track and focused.

That was me before Hannah.

Now everything I do is intentional. In the most basic terms, it is always asking, *What do I want to do here? What decision am I going to make?* Then I follow through.

Before we go any further, let's acknowledge the roadblock that's in all our way: there will be times when we feel like we don't have a choice. But it's not true. It's the crap our minds make up. Learning how to make the best choices despite outside forces is how we make our maps. We can't let fear, insecurity, and naysayers own our journeys. If you're not happy or fulfilled, you're not living your one life. Period.

MAKING YOUR BUSINESS PLAN WORK

Whether it is business or your approach to life, engaging the **Make Your Own Map** is nuanced, so I've made a three-part formula for you to follow. You need to know how to:

- Play to win, not to avoid losing.
- Be bold. Be different. Be willing to not be liked.
- Live for a purpose bigger than you .

Let me walk you through each component.

PLAY TO WIN, NOT TO AVOID LOSING

Taking life as it comes is playing to avoid losing. It is settling—doing everything you can to play it safe and minimize risk. Many of the choices you make will fall into this camp, and that's okay. But you don't want to live there.

Many people take more safe bets than inspired risks. They do what the people around them do and suppress what they want to fly under the radar in the land of normal.

Playing to win is the opposite. It's when you choose the inspired path. You take risks. You go for the epic path. You do what you want, believe in it, and stand for it, no matter what other people think.

Sticking with car analogies, playing to win is like shifting gears on the car you're driving. It's a success mindset strategy that amplifies your approach to life altogether. Think about it this way: you can make a map no matter what you're driving, but if you know how to operate your vehicle, you'll be able to travel that map much more efficiently.

Hannah's birth shifted me into overdrive. Before her, I was just existing. I was playing in life to avoid losing. And my life matched that attitude. I had a small apartment and a sales job where I earned very little. My mindset wasn't big enough back then for me to own a billion-dollar company. I thought small, and my life reflected my limitations.

You don't have to have a major life change to make an attitude adjustment. At any moment, you can choose. Who are you going to be? You get to choose to play to win or play to avoid losing. Are you going to settle for having a small, middle-of-the-road company, or are you aiming for first in the field?

After my breakdown the night Hannah was born, I hired an attorney and filed for joint custody. That was playing to win. From that moment, I started living more powerfully. Of course, I didn't stay in overdrive all the time, but I did start training myself to get there faster. By the end of this book, you'll be able to get there too. But you must practice playing to win by taking risks and doing what inspires you even if it pisses other people off.

Playing to win feels different. You don't feel like you're settling. When you make a choice and feel excited, lit up, and thrilled about it, then you're playing to win. Anything that makes you feel defeated or resigned is just not it. I saw the difference on my pop's face when I was fourteen years old.

LIFE OR BUSINESS: CHOOSE THE PLAN THAT IS BEST FOR YOU

My dad worked for AT&T, and one day, his office closed. He was given the choice to move and work out of another location or be laid off with no severance. I knew this because my parents were pretty cool with us kids. They never hid their adult conversations. So when they delivered the news, I knew it was coming.

"Jayson, we're moving to North Carolina," my mom said. My dad stood next to her, looking stern but defeated. It's one of the only times I've seen him a bit emotional.

Except I'd been in earshot, down the hall, listening to their entire conversation, and moments earlier this had been their discussion: "Mike thinks we should stay, and I should open a sub shop. We could stay here," my dad said. "You could open a bakery."

His friend, Mike Roberts, ran a video store and pitched my dad on the idea of opening a submarine sandwich joint. He said he'd help, and my mom could open a bakery. With Sherry's Bake Shop,

Billy's Subs, and Mike's video store in place, the three of them would own the strip. Wafts of cookies and subs would permeate and mix with the popcorn fumes of the video store, and customers would be lured from one shop to the next.

I heard the pitch of my mom's voice rise as they talked about it. She was pleased my dad thought her baking was good enough for a shop. They were both inspired—for about ten seconds. Then practicality kicked in.

"But Jeremy and Jessi have asthma. Their meds are expensive," he continued. "And you really only have ten more years left at AT&T," my mom said.

So we moved. And not because it was the better choice. North Carolina was a downgrade. We went from a house to our baby-blue trailer that didn't even have bricks around it for the longest time. Being moved to a brand-new place, I felt just like the exposed rusted underbelly of that blue trailer.

Because of fear, my dad chose not to play to win. He played to not lose. He was playing safe, and that's okay. I saw that, and I think even then, it had an impact. But I didn't appreciate this difference when kids at school noticed my Tommy Hilfiger shirt was a fake and started making fun of me. From there, the judgments came: "Oh, you live in Southbrook—in the trailer park."

I knew I was being selfish, but I wanted to stay with my friends in Arizona. I came with a style and attitude that didn't mix with the NC crowd. I dressed like most of my Arizona friends: Dickies and a bandana.

In Arizona, no one was judgmental about where you lived or how much money you had. But people in North Carolina cared about things like what kind of car I drove, which at the time was a $300, multicolored, '84 Dodge Lancer with insulation falling out of the top.

For a kid who used that car to help his family by delivering papers with his dad at night—a son who watched his dad struggle all his life—this was culture shock, and unfortunately, it led to my eventual expulsion from school after struggling to fit in resulted in several altercations and fistfights.

Benji was the one friend I made. This was the same guy who came with me to the hospital the day Hannah was born, and he was there when I first started to make my own map.

My mom loves to play gin rummy and spades. Mom, Benji, and I would often be at our trailer playing cards. While one of us shuffled, Benji and I would talk business. I remember telling my mom around the cusp of turning sixteen, "Me and Ben, we're going to start our own operation one day. We're going to drive a Winnebago around, and then we're going to travel the world."

My parents never did anything like that. The first time they left American soil was in 2019. I took them out of America and flew them over to Turks and Caicos for a holiday.

Despite my parents pressuring me to "finish school, go to college, and get a 'real' job," I knew it was not my path. I ended up becoming a teenage dad and, like my father, was motivated to work to provide. That motivation was ignited by my wife's family, who also judged me for where I lived. Their comments hurt my wife, inspiring a "sick motivation" in me to do whatever I had to be in a financial position to one day handle all our expenses.

Playing to win, not to avoid losing, might look different from one person to the next. It might be changing careers and going back to school when you're forty. It might look like starting a dream business and building it in the evenings while you earn a paycheck at a job you hate until you can quit. It might look like picking up the phone to call a person you think is way more successful than you.

Whatever it is, playing to win is making sure you're cool with the route you're on. Do you want a life that is safe, where you settle, and that is mediocre? Or a life where you play full out, 100 percent, even when you're scared? While you might have more moments of fear on the map you're making, you'll be way more fulfilled if you set out with this mindset.

BE BOLD. BE DIFFERENT. BE WILLING TO BE NOT LIKED.

Since your map is an expression of you, your journey should be as unique as your DNA. Living by the **Make Your Own Map** principle means you must be willing to do the opposite of what others around you are doing—which also means not being liked by everyone.

You might make people angry. You might look like a fool. You might make a mistake. But you'll learn what you're made of. You'll also see how much more people respect you. Plus, you'll be way happier because you're living life on your terms.

So how do you override the discomfort of being bold? Know what you stand for and take bold actions from your place of truth. Not being liked is only tough for a person when they are not secure about who they are.

PAUSE HERE. HOW ARE YOU IN YOURSELF?

Doing what everybody else does doesn't make you stand out—but that's not actually a good thing. They're all the same. Same never gets anyone anywhere. Elon Musk is successful because he's different. Bill Gates is different. Jeff Bezos is fucking different!

Owning your differences is a skill that, like any skill, you practice. You consult with yourself on what you want and believe you should do, and then you commit to taking action.

Two years after Hannah was born, I started being more of a pedal-to-the-metal kind of guy. Life was getting better too. I made more bold moves. I started winning in business. I earned enough to buy a house. I showed myself and everyone around me that I was finally doing what I wanted.

One day, out of the blue, I asked Liz to marry me.

Her family still didn't want us to be together. We fought a lot. My relationship with her parents was up and down, and Hannah was being shuffled between us. One day we were playing house, and then we weren't. One week we were on. The next week we were off.

But I was twenty years old and starting to experience some success. So I decided that I was ready to buy a house—and I called Liz up first.

"Look, I'm going to buy this house. I don't want to live there myself. You and Hannah should move in with me. Let's get married."

Bold. Different. Willing to not be liked.

Bam! I did it.

Liz got off the phone, called and dumped her boyfriend (we were in an off-again period), and pulled up to my apartment building an hour later. She was in everyday clothes—a black t-shirt and khaki-colored pants—and so was I. We went down to the justice of peace right then and got married. Bam! Just like that.

Afterward, I told Liz we were going to see her mom. Her mom still hated me, but I looked her mom in the face, and I told her how it was going to be. "Look, this is my family now," I said. "If you want anything to do with us, you're going to respect me. This is what this is."

Then I told her I had bought us a house and we were going to move in when it was ready, but in the meantime, we needed to stay with her. I had to leave my apartment rental. I continued, "So I'm going to live here together with my wife and my kid for a few weeks until the house is finished. Is that a problem?"

It wasn't. I learned that day that if you stand up for what you believe and ask for what you want, people respect that. They may not like it or agree, but they'll respect it. And that's a big deal. I earned my mother-in-law's respect that day.

The bigger deal? I respected myself. That's what being bold and standing in your values gets you.

LIVE FOR SOMETHING BIGGER THAN YOU

Being bold is not always easy. I get it. So I have one final practice to make you push past the fear: live for a why that's bigger than you.

I believe a CEO should be very involved in the community, and not only be involved, but be passionate about it. If you're going to employ people in a local area and you're going to serve customers in that area, you need to serve the community and be a voice. You're the leader of your organization, and you need to bring that out to the people in the locations you're at. You want to make a difference, not just for your business but for the community. I think we've done a great job with that at POWERHOME SOLAR. Whether it be supporting "Military Makeover" by giving deserving veterans a free solar energy system, donating thousands to the GivePower Foundation in support of providing clean water to people around the world, or in outreach efforts like Gobble Gobble Give or Toys for Tots, we want to make a difference in everything we do.

On my podcast *True Underdog*, I interview the world's most successful millionaires and billionaires, and I get a lot of questions from entrepreneurs starting out who think the wrong way about success.

"I just want to be rich. How do I become a multimillionaire like you, Jayson?" they ask.

That is the wrong question. And it's coming from the wrong mindset. Think that way, and it might make you rich. But it won't get you to fulfillment. You must think bigger.

The question to ask here is: how are you going to change the world? Can you create a successful business that also makes the world a better place?

People struggle with the **Make Your Own Map** principle when they don't have an exciting destination that they want to get to. It doesn't have to be an objectively big goal, but it does have to be bigger than you. At the end of this chapter, you'll be asked to seriously think about your destination and commit to it.

You'll know you've landed on the right "something" by how it feels. Think of when you get excited because you're driving to the airport for a trip, a sports game to see your favorite team play, or out on a date? You feel like you just can't get there soon enough. You're energized. All you can think about is what's to come.

That's the kind of feeling you want to have when you consider the destination you're heading toward or the company you want to create. Where are you going? What's your why? And most importantly, who (other than you) is it for?

Everything is easy when you live for a cause—something greater than yourself. You'll blow yourself away with where you get to in life when you do this.

When you live for any mission greater than yourself—when your purpose is for other people—here's what happens:

- You work much harder.
- You achieve greater outcomes faster (because you're working much harder).
- You feel inspired, alive, and energized.
- You tap into a level of performance that you didn't know existed.
- You drop your own petty reasons for not having what you want.
- You drop your BS excuses.

Hannah helped me stop thinking only about me. It was Liz, Hannah, and me. And then we added three more to the Waller pack: my daughter Mackenzie, her sister Londyn, and then my son Christian. And now Hannah is married, and I have my two grandkids.

There's also my business partner Kevin Klink, my executive team, the employees we pay, and every person who puts our solar panels on their house. I've never stopped living for my family and the people I serve.

Whatever motivates you is the destination you design your map or business plan around. The key is that it's got to be selfless. You can't do something for just yourself. It's got to be bigger than you.

For some people, it's as simple as wanting to help their parents out or care and provide for a kid. There are doctors who want to save lives, teachers who want to teach, and first responders who want to be there whenever someone needs them. Those purposes are all bigger than the people themselves. For me, early on it was to provide and give my daughter the best life she could possibly have.

Remember, her life started pretty screwed up. Her family was a mess from the moment her mom had to hide from her dad in the hospital. I had a lot of ground to make up. I had to make that better. I lived for her.

Success isn't being rich or famous—it's making an impact in life for other people besides ourselves. That is when we feel joy. That is when we find success.

LIFE SHOULD BE A JOY RIDE—EVEN FOR UNDERDOGS

It's the little decisions in life, the left and right turns, that add up to big wins and the coolest, most mind-blowing destinations Living for a why greater than myself is how I won the Ernst & Young Entrepreneur of the Year Award in 2019. Success always follows when you live for a why greater than you.

In our business, we're up for all kinds of awards. Not that I don't care about awards, but I am more focused on building value in the company than plaques with my name on them. I had no clue what the EY award was or that it was important. Then one week before the event, Liz and I were hosting a couples' game night. I'm friends with a couple of Lions football players, and we have them and a couple of neighbors all over after the kids are in bed to play games and enjoy each other's company.

My buddy Brian works for Ernst and Young and told me he had heard about my nomination. "Hey, man, congrats on the nomination for the Entrepreneur of the Year Award for the Southeast!"

"Oh, thanks. You heard about that?" I asked. My team had posted it on social media, but I didn't think anyone really noticed.

"Yeah. You going to the banquet thing?"

"Nah, man."

"You're not going to meet the judges to try to win?" he asked.

"Nope."

Three months before the award is given publicly at a fancy gala, all the judges and nominees gather. Each nominee must present to a panel and state why they should be the winner.

"Dude, this is a big deal. Daymond John from *Shark Tank* won it once. You need to go to this," he said.

"Shit."

I texted Roger, my marketing manager, and told him I needed to go. The event was one week away, and Roger made a handful of calls to important EY people to claim my spot.

Then he booked me a flight, claimed my seat at the dinner, and met me in Charlotte with a manila folder full of information. The brief explained who was going to be there, including twenty-five other nominees, and what I needed to do. He prepared me for a cocktail party that was taking place before the judges panel the next day.

I was a little intimidated when Roger and I went to the party, which is unusual. I had to make a quick decision to be there. I had made a sharp right turn on my map, and it all happened fast.

As Roger and I were mingling and talking to the nominees, I noticed they were all dry-run pitching to each other why they should win. And the stories were mostly angled around MBAs, awards, and dollars made.

We made our way to Chevenry Arnold, who runs the program for EY out of the Southeast, as a TV screen behind us showed a sports anchor talking about the NBA draft. "There is talk of Zion going back to Duke," the anchor reported.

I made a comment about it, and Chevenry asked me if that was where I went to college. "I didn't go to college," I said.

"Oh, you're the one," she said.

"The one what?"

"You're one of the first nominees for the EY award who didn't go to college."

The difference between me and the other nominees was that I didn't have an MBA. When Chevenry told me, I had a moment of panic. *There is no way I'll win,* I thought for a split second. Then I decided the only choice I had was to own my adversity. It was the best decision I could have made.

The next day, I had to go into an interview first with ten judges in one room and then another room with another ten judges. Later, when Roger called me to see how it went, I said, "There's not a thing I could have done different, Rog. I dropped the mic."

I chose the moment. I led with all the shit that made me an unlikely candidate—an underdog which also made me the best candidate there ever was for that award. Because I made my map. I decided. I committed. I spoke boldly. I was there for my family and my team and didn't care what anyone thought, so I spoke my truth.

I told them I should win the Entrepreneur of the Year because I didn't go to college. Because nothing was handed to me. Because I bootstrapped from nothing. Because this was the third business I had built. Because I sacrificed my home and didn't get paid for almost two years when I built POWERHOME. I told them to double down on betting on me and this company because we were building a movement. Bam!

Three months later, in a suit and bowtie with all my partners and Liz around a banquet table with a giant candelabra, I panicked. I'd been so confident until that point. I was telling everyone I had it in the bag. I was going to win. I freaked out. "What if I don't win?" I said to Liz.

"That wouldn't be good," she said.

But then they called my name, and it was surreal and freaking cool. I'd made it to one cool destination, all by staying true to myself, my family, and my map. I want the same for you.

You get to say how your life goes. You get to make your own map. Start now.

CHAPTER CHALLENGE

MAKE YOUR OWN MAP

Take reflection time to think about your life both personally and professionally. Use this section as a workbook to get things out of your head and into the word on paper—it makes a difference. Go through this series of questions, and be brutally honest with your answers. Write full paragraphs or just bullet point your answers, but get it on paper. Then rip this page out of the book and hang it up somewhere you will see it every day—a bathroom mirror, your refrigerator, or the side of your computer monitor. The location doesn't matter, only that you see it every day. To change your underdog story, you must keep being honest with yourself and where you want to go. Reading the answers to the questions below daily will keep you focused and motivated to make your own map and own your power.

1. On a scale of 1-10, how satisfied are you with your current life? **Circle one.**

1 2 3 4 5 6 7 8 9

*no 10—you can always live bigger.

2. Do you feel in charge of your life? **Circle one.**

Yes / No

3. Are there things you want to achieve that seem out of reach?

....

....

....

....

4. Rate your attitude/mindset. How does this attitude make a difference in the life that you are currently leading? **Circle one and describe.**

    Awesome → Bored → Negative → Wishy-washy
    → Growth-oriented → Frustrated

....

....

....

....

5. Are you playing to win or not to lose? **List examples.**

....

....

....

....

6. What, if anything, would you like to change about your life?

....

....

....

....

Remember, make your own map, and adjust it as often as necessary to get where you want to go. When you set a new goal, create a plan to make it happen that includes what decisions and/or changes you need to make to reach your goal. If these changes involve your career or business, don't be afraid to radically revise your business plan in terms of execution and results—just don't lose sight of where you are going.

Making your own map and following it to achieve your goals requires that you act, evaluate the results of that action, and implement again as many times as needed to make it happen. The key to taking action in very decisive moments is asking this very important question: *Is this really what I want to do?*

If you're ready to own your power and take control of your life both in business and personally, you need massive accountability. To keep yourself accountable, share your actions with me and everyone who is reading this book. Post a picture of yourself taking the action or a picture of your answers to the questions above to show and inspire others to do the work too. Use hashtags #OYPmakeyourownmap #OwnYourPower or #JaysonWaller.

NOTES:

https://www.indeed.com/career-advice/career-development/
parts-to-a-business-plan.

CHAPTER TWO

PRINCIPLE #2—THERE'S NO ELEVATOR IN LIFE—YOU'VE GOTTA TAKE THE STAIRS

When I opened my first home security business in 2005, I ran it from a 100-square-foot office that was also my bedroom. The room—a.k.a. my first office—was so small that two people couldn't stand shoulder to shoulder across it. All I had was a tileboard from Home Depot that I got for twenty-five dollars, a black magic marker, and a scuffed-up secondhand table and chair. I didn't have a fax machine, a computer, or much of anything else.

I hung the tileboard in the hallway and used it to schedule the installs as we booked them. I spent hours standing in that hall working on the tileboard and getting annoyed with Liz every time she needed to shimmy by me to go to the bathroom.

My business partner then, who is still with me today, was Kevin Klink. I love the guy. Our business was growing, but it was slow. Almost every week, I would drive to our customers to pick up signed contracts for the alarm systems my installers were putting in. Then I would mail them right away to fund payroll. Every month, it was the same routine. I'd pull up to whatever address was next on my clipboard. I'd flag down my guy and double-check that the information was complete so we didn't have any issues processing payments. Anything missing could cause payment delays.

Once I'd collected enough signed contracts to meet payroll, I'd head to the nearest post office to mail them in.

I was working for Verizon as a sales guy too, all the while growing this home security business on the side from my home. We were making progress, but it was a slow climb. Life was nuts. Most people would have quit.

Building two multimillion-dollar businesses and one-billion-dollar business teaches you the importance of small wins. I didn't wake up one morning and have these thriving businesses. I did, however, go to sleep night after night counting my small wins, hoping they would pay off big. Some days you're making progress, but it's so small you barely notice it. Back then, our business was growing slowly but with integrity.

At first, I ran all the flyer appointments. Then it grew to a team, and we went door to door to hang flyers, which I got made at a five-cent photocopy place. They were crappy, but it was all I could afford, and they got the job done.

If we stopped by your place, you would come home after work around five to find a door hanger that said:

> ## FREE ALARM SYSTEM WITH INSTALLATION AND YOUR CHOICE OF CRAFTSMAN GARAGE DOOR OPENER INSTALLED OR $150 GIFT CARD TO HOME DEPOT.
>
> ## MONITORING IS ONE DOLLAR A DAY. CALL FOR DETAILS.

You would call, and I'd answer. "Yeah, you want that garage opener. Great! We're going to get you the alarm system and the garage door. I'll come out and meet you. It's a dollar a day for the monitoring. Installation is free. How about I come and see you this afternoon? I'll be there at six."

This was a good way to build sales, which is a good way to build a business. Why? Because the customer was getting a product that the owner was selling. It was integrity driven.

Kevin and I wanted to scale faster. We put more flyers out. We got more calls.

Since you can only put so many flyers out and take so many calls, we started looking for people to knock on doors. Our plan was simple. Hire sales managers and have them ride with me so I could train them on how to knock on doors. Then the sales manager would train the new hires. Simple.

In those early slow-growth days, since my bedroom was my office, we would meet our potential hires at our local Chili's restaurant. They would ask where our office was, and I had to say, "We don't have one, but you've got to trust me."

This sharpened my skills to be able to sell someone the dream of what I envisioned for the company, without an office, without real flyers, without business cards or even a computer. I had to sell the pieced-together business like it was the most solid business ever.

At the beginning, I sold accounts and scheduled the installs. Sometimes I delivered the equipment, thanked the customer in person, and shook their hands. Those are the steps you have to take when building your business. There is no elevator. You must grind it out.

We scaled with van teams. And eventually, Kevin and I thought we were going to be okay. I still couldn't leave my job at Bell Atlantic Verizon, but we were almost there.

We eventually grew enough to get a small office and hire more people. Six months later we got a bigger office. Then after that an even bigger office. It was one step at a time. Take the steps. One by one. Get to the next level, each time becoming more professional, improving the operation, scaling, and getting better. Then more staff and computers. Branding. Even a marketing wrap on your car.

When I started my first business, in that 100-square-foot room, I was taking it one stair step at a time. I kept on climbing up the stairs, even if I stumbled backward at times. No shortcuts.

You don't open a company one day and spend a million dollars to get it off the ground. Not at the beginning. You just take it day by day. Do the work. And then one day you get there. We started from a tileboard, and we grew it step by step to $13 million.

BE CAREFUL WHO YOU HIRE

It is important I don't gloss over a critical point here. Let me be candid. In all this growth, we stumbled a couple of times. To be honest, we got greedy.

You can't blame us. It's human nature. Everyone wants the quick-fix diet, to win the lottery, or to learn the secret sales hack that brings leads in faster. Kevin and I were no different. It was around this time that the **There's No Elevator in Life—You've Gotta Take the Stairs** principle started to take form.

Rather than developing our own sales teams, van teams, and promotion teams, we took a shortcut, ignoring best practices for hiring personnel. We hired what's called a "summer program." These were teams of seasonal transient salespeople—I call them locusts now—who travel from city to city selling home security during the summer months. And we hired a bunch of these guys to sell for us.

"Our business will explode," Kevin and I kept saying to each other.

We paid these guys top dollar. Their ads said they had worked for some big-name brands, so we thought bringing them to the Carolinas to sell for us was what we needed. Bring them in, and business will boom.

Our dumbass plan didn't work because they had been trained by four other companies. They didn't eat, sleep, and bleed our brand. In fact, they didn't care about it at all. Their sales results were garbage, and we paid them way too much for it. We even paid for their apartments so they had nice places to stay. (They trashed them.) Our profit margins shrunk, and they tainted our name in the process. There were good reasons those guys bounced around and didn't have full-time jobs. We realized this too late, and it hurt.

Have you ever seen a farmer's field that has been hit by locusts? The short-horned grasshoppers decimate it. Unsated, the locusts move on to the next field to consume, always leaving destruction in their wake.

If you've hired someone who's only there for money, you have the wrong employee.

The worst part is that we'd had a plan to develop and train our own salespeople, but we put it aside to get to success faster using the locusts.

Making that choice was stepping away from the goal, away

from the journey, away from the map. We got off the stairs that we'd steadily climbed, step by step. The elevator looked fancy, faster, and easier. We didn't get far. Eventually, we went back to square one and had to build back after the mess the locusts left us in.

If you cheat the system, rush the process, or otherwise try to progress faster, it'll never work.

Sure, you might snag short-term wins, but you'll miss out on the skills you need to develop. This approach is about integrity and the value of putting in the work. There's value to following a tried-and-true process in life, even if results are slow.

It's normal to be tempted to rush. But there is a step-by-step process to everything you do. Don't let your emotions get the best of you. Stick. To. The. Stairs.

INCREMENTAL PROGRESS IS EVERYTHING

What if you got 1 percent better each day?

Would that be hard? Probably not.

Would you notice a difference? Probably not.

Fast forward one year, 365 days later, and you would see a 365 percent improvement. Unfortunately, there is no way to fast forward through those increments. We must trust the process.

Building anything that's worthwhile takes time. It might be building a business, getting a college degree, or raising a human until they are self-sufficient. Like watching the grass grow, it might seem like today is no different than yesterday, but it is. You've learned something or you've moved a little closer every day.

Remember the tortoise and the hare story from when you were a kid? The hare makes fun of the tortoise for being too slow. "Do you ever get anywhere?" the hare asks the tortoise. But then the two of them race, and the tortoise wins. Slow and steady wins the damn race, right?

People tend to forget this basic tenet. We want what we want, and we want it now.

The **There's No Elevator in Life—You've Gotta Take the Stairs** principle is about not skipping any steps, like we did when we thought we could fast-track our sales process. It is about taking complete actions even when you're experiencing slow, incremental progress. Don't look for a quick way to achieve an outcome through half-assed shortcuts. That's cheating, and it won't get you very far. Sometimes, as we learned, it can set you back quite a bit.

Sometimes skipping steps looks like quitting way too early. "Oh,

I'm not making money yet. I'm going to quit," entrepreneurs will sometimes say to me. Impatience takes people out. They try to take the elevator. They try to achieve what they want faster with a quick-fix solution or quit when they are making progress because they aren't celebrating the little wins. If you're a little further than you were last week, it's not time to give up.

I launched my first business from my bedroom. In 2002, when I was young and didn't know what the hell I was doing, I filed bankruptcy. I worked with no paycheck for a span of almost two years when I built POWERHOME SOLAR. The money I did make I put back into the business. I've overcome lawsuits. I've dealt with employee theft. My current business has had to overcome tax credits that vanished in certain states. There was no get-rich-quick scheme or magic formula. I took the stairs.

Today, I run a billion-dollar business, which qualifies me to be a business judge on the Bloomberg Business show, 2 *Minute Drill,* where I give advice to newbie entrepreneurs.

I've had a lot of good experiences and plenty of bad ones too. I'm an expert and give advice today. But you know what? I'm still climbing stairs. They never end.

> **The little wins add up, though sometimes you barely notice them. Look closely. Zoom into your *now* moment, and track your micro metrics to motivate yourself to keep going. Don't let the way you feel dictate what you do. You will get there. Take the steps one at a time, and don't be greedy. The elevator might be faster in the short term, but in the long term, you'll just screw yourself out of success.**

When I started POWERHOME, I doubled down on the **There's No Elevator in Life—You've Gotta Take the Stairs** principle. I even replicated the alarm business startup process. I went out and bought a tileboard and used manila folders to schedule the solar installs.

I remember we even grew to two tileboards, and then we started using a solar panel as our board.

I did everything. I called customers. I wrote up proposals. I closed deals. I took measurements. You name it. As a result, I know the company's business inside and out. I know everyone's job. I could step into anyone's role and do the job. That is taking the stairs. When I motivate our sales guys today, I've been where they are.

The **There's No Elevator in Life—You've Gotta Take the Stairs** principle has also helped me get through the tough times. It's a principle that anyone can use to be resilient. When it feels like I'm going backward, if I have evidence that I am not, however small, it gives me hope, and I keep moving forward.

Sometimes you need to pause on the stairs. Sometimes you need to take one or two steps back. That's okay too. Failures happen. So you pause or step back, and then you reorient and step forward again.

I've full-on tripped and crashed down the stairs like a stuntman on fire, and I got up and said, "That was a bad fall." As long as you're not stagnating or going backward for too long, it's okay. If you're making progress day by day, you're good. The **There's No Elevator in Life—You've Gotta Take the Stairs** principle reminds you to be patient and keep moving forward, bit by bit. Don't get ahead of yourself like the hare. Be the tortoise. Choose slow and steady. There's value in the process.

QUICK WINS ARE EMOTIONAL SHORT-TERM FIXES

When I was nineteen, I landed a job at First Union. Eight months in, on what was otherwise a typical day in the office, my boss, John McKinley, invited me to his office for some straight talk.

"Jayson, do you or don't you have a college degree?"

John had caught me. I had lied to the human resources recruiter. To get the job, I faked my resume. I took the elevator, not the stairs.

You see, to apply for the job at First Union Bank, applicants had to have a two-year degree. I didn't have one, but I knew I could sell. So I pimped out my resume. I felt high and mighty the day I typed "Sales Management Degree—UNC Charlotte" under the education section. *I'm a genius. This will totally work.*

And my plan did work—at least at first.

First Union hired me as one of their sales associates. My job was to call customers and upsell them to savings accounts. I spent time on the phone, which I was good at. I'm a talker. People who know me best know this is one of the reasons I'm great at sales.

"I see you've got $10,000 in your savings account," I'd say. "What if we move this to a money market account? You get 3.5 percent interest on your money. And we'll waive all the fees."

I was young and hungry. I was blowing the other sales reps out of the water. My sales skills were next-level. Admittedly, I had a bit of an ego about it too. I'd faked my resume. It had worked. No one knew the truth, and now there I was crushing it.

I figured the lie was behind me. Then on a day like any other, the HR manager pulled me into her office for a chat.

"We called UNC Charlotte, and they said they couldn't find your degree," she said.

Oh no! They had caught me. Shit! Think fast, man. You can come up with an excuse. You're a sales rock star.

"Did you look under William?" I asked. William is my middle name. It was a quick recovery.

"No, we looked under Jayson."

"Oh, you see, that's the problem. It's under William."

Safe. Bam! Close one. Again, I thought it was behind me, but it wasn't.

By that time, I was the number-one sales guy. What were they going to do, fire me? I was winning them awards. They gave me a plaque by week two. The top loan officer for Wachovia took me golfing. I broke records. So I kept going.

But my fake-ass resume situation wasn't over. This is when John got involved. I came clean that day. I couldn't lie to John.

"Why would you lie?" he asked me.

"You guys wouldn't have hired me if I didn't," I said. "And you wouldn't be the number-one manager right now if I wasn't on your team."

Luckily, I got to keep the job. And while this might seem like a victory story in which I took the elevator—where I cheated the system and won—it wasn't. It was a short-term victory. It always is when you don't take the stairs. My undoing as a sales guy in that job was because I didn't learn the step-by-step process. Yes, I had passion. Yes, I was a great sales guy. But eventually I fell behind. I didn't have the experience, background, and knowledge that the other associates did. And I had a smudge on my name at First Union because I'd falsified my application.

Taking the elevator can lead to short-term wins, but with that comes long-term setbacks and struggles. This is true of any process. While a strict diet will help a person lose weight fast, they'll likely put the weight back on or gain more because of the stress they put on their body.

Anyone who sells themselves well on a resume, like I did, will suffer because they don't have the hard skills they need to do the job. And how many couples move in, get married, or have kids without going through the time, process, and work it takes to make sure they are committed to the same type of life and they don't just think the other person is hot?

It's never smart to take the elevator. Take the stairs. Incremental progress is key.

MICRO FOCUS AND USE METRICS OVER FEELINGS

In 2020, I sat down for a podcast interview with Jim McKelvey, who is one of the world's top business innovators and the author of the book *The Innovation Stack: Building an Unbeatable Business One Crazy Idea at a Time.*

Whether you've read his book or recognize the name, I guarantee you have used his product. McKelvey and his business partner, Jack Dorsey, who was the Co-Founder of Twitter, invented the Square card reader. If you've purchased an item from a small business owner and swiped your card on a mini white square at checkout, you've used their invention.

McKelvey came up with the idea because he lost a sale when he couldn't accept American Express cards in 2009. Frustrated by the challenge of accepting credit card payments along with the high cost, he teamed up with Jack Dorsey, and together they launched Square. The problem they would solve revolved around the fact that major credit card companies were profiting off small businesses at a rate forty-five times higher than big billion-dollar corporations. McKelvey knew this problem was a big issue for a lot of people. It was a great reason to start a company. This innovative startup enabled small businesses to accept credit card payments on their mobile phones.

Square's innovative solution transformed the payments market-place. The company surpassed $1 billion in subscription revenue in 2019. They got there one stair at a time.

McKelvey and Dorsey had a big dream but a micro focus. To build the Square card reader, they started at zero with just an idea. They invented a new product by solving a chain of problems. It's a process McKelvey called the Innovation Stack method, which is a powerful concept for startups, based on the idea that companies should stack interlinking innovation as part of their infrastructure because doing so makes them more likely to succeed than startups that don't stack.

"If you try to do something new, you will encounter a series of new problems," McKelvey told me. "The solution to one problem leads to another problem, sometimes several."

The problem-solution-problem chain repeats until you end up with a collection of both independent and interlocking inventions. Or you fail.

Think of the Wright brothers' invention of the airplane. It's a great example McKelvey uses in his book. First, they had to figure out how to get a giant machine to lift off and fly. Then once it was in the air, they had a new problem: how do you steer? They had to figure that out too. And they had to start by being willing to not know how what they were doing was going to play out.

McKelvey's journey to invent the Square card reader is like what you want to do when you take the stairs. You have a big dream, which is someplace you want to get to in life. But to get there you must start from where you're at.

So you take the first step and then the next. That's it. It's about micro focus and tracking your metrics each step of the way to monitor your progress.

The question to ask is: am I improving here?

The best way to prove it to yourself is to measure your progress and track the metrics, and don't pay too much attention to your feelings if you are positively moving in the right direction. Remember if you look too far ahead, it's easy to get impatient. Don't focus on what you don't have.

Let's say you're building a business. You might have moments when you're frustrated because you're not as successful as you'd like to be. It's easy to get caught up in the outcomes you've failed to achieve and feel like a loser.

If you think it's going to take forever until you do $5 million in sales, that attitude won't get you far. You might have setbacks, but if you look at your small wins and your progress over the last few months, if you're trending up, it's easy to assess whether you're making headway or not. If you take the longer view, you can see the curve of improvement. Up close, it will look like you're up one month and down the next. Over time you can map the data points and see the incremental progress.

At POWERHOME SOLAR, 2020 was a record-breaking year. But in November, our revenue took a nosedive. It was bad. I questioned the leadership team on why this happened. "It's election month," they told me. They also said it was because of COVID-19 and Thanksgiving. My argument was that we knew it was an election month. We knew Thanksgiving was here. We knew about COVID-19. "We have to do better in December," I told them.

Compared to other months, this month was an outlier. It's okay to take a step backward on the stairs. Setbacks happen. It's not always forward progress every single time. Taking the stairs also means when you get knocked down you get back up and keep going.

So to know if you're on the right path, you look at the three-month pattern and consider the small wins. And when you do this, you always focus on metrics, not feelings. Anything you can physically measure or count is a metric. Dollars and cents in a bank account. Numbers on a scale, if you're tracking weight. The number of kisses your wife gives you might tell you how satisfied she is with your relationship. All of these are tangible metrics. They aren't how you feel. They are known quantities. You must focus on the facts, not the stories in your head, to know whether you're making progress.

CHART 1—SETTING METRICS TO COUNTERBALANCE FEELINGS

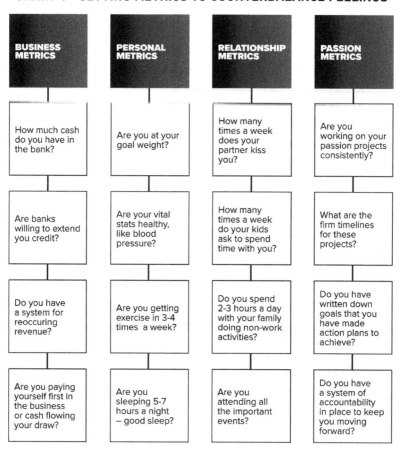

BUSINESS METRICS	PERSONAL METRICS	RELATIONSHIP METRICS	PASSION METRICS
How much cash do you have in the bank?	Are you at your goal weight?	How many times a week does your partner kiss you?	Are you working on your passion projects consistently?
Are banks willing to extend you credit?	Are your vital stats healthy, like blood pressure?	How many times a week do your kids ask to spend time with you?	What are the firm timelines for these projects?
Do you have a system for reoccuring revenue?	Are you getting exercise in 3-4 times a week?	Do you spend 2-3 hours a day with your family doing non-work activities?	Do you have written down goals that you have made action plans to achieve?
Are you paying yourself first in the business or cash flowing your draw?	Are you sleeping 5-7 hours a night – good sleep?	Are you attending all the important events?	Do you have a system of accountability in place to keep you moving forward?

*The above is an example of a simple chart you can create around metrics for every aspect of your life. When creating your own version of the chart, make sure that every metric you list down a category is 100 percent fact-based, with no room for emotion to sneak in. Clearly, you get very detailed with this chart and break your business into sales, profit, capital, payroll, and so on as long as every metric flowing down the category can be answered with a yes or no or a specific data point that can be fact-checked.

PATIENCE ALWAYS WINS!

I see it all the time among entrepreneurs, people in relationships, even my sales reps. They say, "I'm not seeing the results fast enough," and they quit too soon because they feel like shit. We all have bad months, bad weeks, bad days. It happens. Nothing is ever a smooth climb.

The plan is to strive for perfection, but don't get caught up in the one massive metric you are trying to get to. It's not going to happen overnight. If you're trying to lose fifty pounds, it's not smart to focus on that number if it's only week one of a new regime. Instead, focus on losing two pounds week by week. Slow gains matter. If you're on an upward trajectory with your progress, you take the next step.

When you're accomplishing anything, treat it like a game. Let's say it's football. There are four quarters in a year of business, and the same is true in a football game.

If you are down after two quarters but you score enough points in the last two quarters of the game, then you win. Look at the situation positively and track the metrics. That's how you're going to progress. That's taking the stairs.

I've had bad months. I've had bad quarters. And I've had bad years. But I've never had a year go backward.

Always ask: what is this moment?

If I'm in December, I'm focused on December. November is behind me. My eyes are forward for a reason. I'm not looking at November. If it was a bad month, screw November. That shit's behind me. Today, I'm focused on December. And then you grade your fourth quarter. How did you do? And if you failed to reach your target in the four quarters, damn it, then you're looking at January to have a good month so you can set up to have a good first quarter and win.

Don't let a bad day (or week or month) control you. Every now and then, you're going to get a loss, but if you have more wins than losses, you're making progress. You're climbing that staircase.

It is okay to slow down. You have time. Be patient.

When you take the stairs, there's an amortization effect. Success gets easier and faster because you've put in the work, time, and effort. You don't get that when you use a quick fix in anything.

Trust the process. Keep walking up the stairs. The moment you cheat, you get off your path, your vision, your map, and you're done.

ARE YOU AGB?

AGB is an acronym I live by. It stands for Always Getting Better. It's one tenet I live by to remind myself to grow each day. Remember it. AGB.

I have a rule in relationships: if the good days outnumber the bad, we're good. When the bad days outnumber the good, we need to talk.

The rule applies to all areas of life. If there are more wins than losses, you keep going and focus on the wins. Develop ways to keep track of your business's growth. Don't dwell on the losses. Keep stepping. You'll get there. One stair at a time. AGB. Always getting better is a simple way to remember to take the stairs, not the elevator.

The world is changing so much that if you don't keep getting better or staying relevant, you become irrelevant.

One of the biggest problems with not taking the steps is that you put yourself in a position where you are held hostage. We'll talk about how to avoid that next.

CHAPTER CHALLENGE

TAKE THE STAIRS

Take reflection time to think about your goals. Use this section to dive deep into the goals you've set and how you will achieve them. Go through this series of questions, and be brutally honest with your answers. Do the work. Then rip this page out of the book and hang it up somewhere you will see it every day—a bathroom mirror, your refrigerator, or the side of your computer monitor. The location doesn't matter, only that you see it every day. To change your underdog story, you must always get better, and to do this, you need incremental progress and the right mindset to keep climbing. Reminding yourself to take the stairs daily will keep you focused and motivated to make your own map and own your power.

1. What is your biggest business goal for the next twelve months?

....

2. What key decisions do you need to make to achieve this goal?

....

....

....

....

3. What two goals can you set every day that move you toward your big twelve-month goal?

....

....

....

....

4. What metrics can you define that prove you are moving toward your big goal?

....

....

....

....

You can repeat this exercise for all your big goals in business and in life. Share the exercise with your employees, and ask them to identify how they will hit their large goals in your company. Make sure to evaluate the effectiveness of the small decisions that you make. Did they move you forward in obtaining your goal? What did you learn from the result? What made it a good decision? What made it a poor one? Ask the important questions.

Focus on incremental wins. Be honest about the set of metrics to measure the growth of your business and your goals overall. Use the metrics to achieve the smaller goals.

And don't forget to celebrate your small wins now or share your next AGB focus by snapping a picture of your answers to the questions above and posting on social media to connect with the Own Your Power community. Use hashtags #OYPNoElevatorInLife, #OwnYourPower, or #JaysonWaller when you share.

CHAPTER THREE

PRINCIPLE #3—NEVER BE HELD HOSTAGE

Do you feel like a victim? Are you doing that to yourself? You must be strategic in life. You must think ahead and build structures around you so you never get stuck in a situation where you can't do what you want to do. No one ever has power over anyone. You need to be smart. You must systemize, skill up, and stand in your values so you don't get in any situation where you are held hostage.

PLAYING THE ROLE OF HOSTAGE

Back in 2008, I had a problem. My sales reps were expensive. They had big egos, and they ran my entire home security business. I learned an important business lesson the hard way: never let anyone get bigger than the system.

I had set up a system that forced me to depend on the sales reps way too much, so I was held hostage by them. Honestly, the entire company was. It was a role I wrote myself into without realizing it.

You see, our company would hire these high-priced sales guys who had a great deal of experience. But every time they had a great week, the next week would be terrible. Why? Because these guys would go out and party or get lazy or comfortable. They would get paid and head to the clubs, where they would blow all their money on table service at the strip club and too much Grey Goose. The following week, revenues would plummet. Then, after a failed week, they would work hard again so sales would skyrocket.

One of the sales guys, Josh, even went missing once for three days. Everyone was worried. "Where is Josh? He was missing for an appointment again," his colleagues were saying. When he finally showed up, he said he'd been kidnapped. Really, he was out partying, chasing women, and doing drugs. I had to fire him.

It was a pattern. I would hire these top sales guys who were young and hungry, and they would get a lot of money in their pocket. They weren't used to it, and they didn't know what to do with it.

I'd built our business operations around the success of sales guys like this with big egos. They didn't care about team success. They were driven by their own wants, needs, and desires. Our company was held hostage by them. No one knew our sales process like they did, not even me. They were hard to replace.

Over my years of managing teams, I've learned how people are very different in what motivates them. Some need to be patted on the back and told, "Good job." Some need to be kicked in the ass and told to work harder. Some need to be told to slow down. When I would praise the wrong salesperson, it went to their head. A lot of these high-priced sales guys started to see themselves as bigger than the company and bigger than me. I created monsters. I put the entire company in a position where they were such an important part of the business that we needed them if we were to survive. They were arrogant assholes, but I couldn't fire them. I was a hostage in my own house.

You can't build a business this way. No one person should ever be bigger than the system. It might be in a business, organization, or any network of people. Groups need rules to function. No one runs the show. Not even the leader at the top.

When you build a business around people, the problem is that their heads can get too big. It can happen with managers or with the C-suite leaders at the top of the org chart. It can happen in personal relationships or families too. When someone has too much power, they become bigger than everyone else, and what they do dictates the future. It's not cool. They hold everyone hostage because they have the most power.

These sales guys pretty much owned me. When I finally did fire them, the company struggled. I needed to make sure it didn't happen again. I didn't want a sales rep's behavior—whether they quit, slacked off, or partied too much—to impact our ability to meet payroll. That went for installers too. If they didn't show up, we didn't make money. Or if an accounting manager quit, there was no one who knew what was going on with the company finances. In other words, I didn't want to be held hostage ever again. Those experiences taught me the **Never Be Held Hostage** principle.

In business and in your personal life, you can't be held hostage. It is not okay if you must surrender to someone or something. For years, I would be stuck in situations where I'd think, *This isn't right. This person is dictating how we pay people. This person is dictating what we're doing here. This person is dictating how we grow. But it's my company. It's my team. It's my family.*

Today, we've got almost 400 sales reps. We still have a few highly paid guys who are at the top. But if one of them is destructive to the business or comes into the office puffing his chest, saying, "You're going to pay me this or else," then I put a stop to it and say, "You've got to go because we've got about 400 other people who can do almost what you can do."

Today our company is not built around one person. We're a team, and we have structures in place. We will not be held hostage. We win and we learn as a team.

BUILD A SMART BUSINESS STRUCTURE

Never Be Held Hostage is about building smart systems to avoid any situation where you feel you can't make the choice you want to make.

In Chapter One, we talked about choice and how you always have a say in how life goes. Here's what's also true about choice: while you always choose what to do about a situation, sometimes your choices are not win-win. And usually, it's because you made bad choices in the lead-up. You put yourself in a hostage situation!

When I had the sales guys, my business was dependent on them, and I didn't like their work ethic, my choices were:

Option 1: Fire them because it aligned with my values, but then deal with the fact that the company was screwed.

Option 2: Keep them and compromise my values temporarily to keep the business afloat.

Neither was a winning solution. But I had done that to myself! I hadn't been thinking smart. I built a business that depended on these guys to sell for us. **Never Be Held Hostage** is about thinking ahead. It's about building structures around you so you don't put yourself in any situation where you are a victim of your own making.

Ultimately, the **Never Be Held Hostage** approach is about personal freedom. How do you make sure you always have winning options? You systemize, skill up, and stand in your values.

Here's what each looks like in action:

SYSTEMIZE

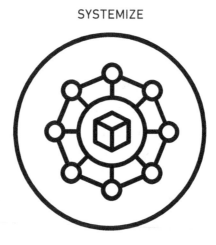

When I say systemize, I mean building safety nets and structures around you that protect you and other people. If you run a business, you should be able to fire a worker who shows up late to appointments without the business failing. In personal relationships, everyone should have the financial resources to walk out of a bad relationship so that any party can leave without serious repercussions. Systemizing means building safety structures for yourself that can keep you from being held hostage by your circumstances.

When you skill up, you are focused on always being the best you can be by learning and getting better. Let's say your boss is a jerk one too many times, and your company's work culture is causing you serious mental distress. It's your responsibility to train yourself. Protect yourself with skills and knowledge. Don't get complacent. If you have enough skill and resources, you can walk out anytime and find another job instead of feeling stuck.

Can you believe that I didn't know what EBITDA was until a couple of years ago? In building a team around me to grow the business, I found people who helped me learn about the importance of EBITDA. You can never be scared of adding talent to your team and finding people who can fill critical roles. I've come to realize that I can't be Superman. You need a team of Avengers to really do everything well so a company like ours can prosper.

Rely on what you believe in. Make decisions using your moral compass. You always know what is right for you. If you are compromising what you believe in, you will feel it instinctually. When you honor your personal values, you can't fail, no matter what. I firmly believe that if you ground yourself in what you know to be true and you let what feels right guide you, you can never go wrong in any situation. How often have you heard someone say, "It didn't feel right, but I did it anyway"? Later they usually end up with a sad story to tell. Remember the story I shared about faking my resume? I went against my value of integrity. And I always felt a little on edge, like I was hiding something, because I was. It was wrong. I knew it. It backfired. I compromised my own values. For me, my values have always guided me to do the right thing. Your intuition will tell you what feels right and what doesn't. Listen to that inner voice. You have an internal compass that's unique to you, and you need to follow it. When you don't know what to do, fall back on your values, and it will become clear what to do next. Let your values guide you, and you will always make the right choices. It doesn't mean that you will avoid mistakes. But it does mean the major decisions you make will be mostly the right ones.

DON'T LIMIT YOUR OPTIONS

Back to the options I had with my sales guy dilemma: fire them and suffer or let them hold me hostage. But what if there was a third option?

Option 3: Do whatever the heck you want. If you've built a no-fail system, there will be few repercussions, and whatever comes up, you'll deal with it. If you check in with your intuition—and use the values sniff test as a safety check—you'll ultimately make the right call, and you'll powerfully deal with any fallout.

You can stand for what you believe in—you don't have to settle for any circumstances you don't like in business or your personal life. You just must be honest about doing the work to support that decision. Don't sugarcoat it. It may suck in the short term, but you will be free and have the control back to follow your own map. A big part of owning your power is not limiting your options and being willing to roll up your sleeves, especially in business, to make a hard decision work out.

I don't know about you, but I'll take option three. But how?

Let's talk about how to follow through on the **Never Be Held Hostage** principle.

SYSTEMS KEEP YOUR BUSINESS SAFE

Think of how a sports team strategizes to increase their odds of winning. They think ahead. They prepare for multiple scenarios. They come to the field, court, or rink with a plan. You can do the same. Find where you're vulnerable; then put systems in place to keep you safe and increase your chances of success.

After the sales guy debacle—which, by the way, happened more than once—I built POWERHOME SOLAR. For my third business, I declared that it wouldn't have one or two rock stars. Instead, we would be a band of brothers and sisters—a rock star team. There would be no individual heroes. We would have to be the Justice League or the Avengers to succeed.

A business needs to be able to both scale and replace its assets, human or otherwise, as it grows. For this to happen, everyone must be interchangeable, like cogs in a machine. No one person, position, or role in the company can be too mission critical.

Now, as I continue to build this business, I do regular audits. I constantly seek to fill gaps in the system. I watch to see if any person has too much responsibility. I always make sure we have a strong bench of players, and I keep a plan B, C, D, and E on deck.

This structure applies to personal relationships too. Everyone involved needs to constantly ensure that their own needs are met and that they are safe to speak their mind at any time.

No person should have power over another, especially because they have access to more resources.

The balance that constitutes a healthy team mentality also contributes to healthy relationships.

Not only should everyone be able to walk away if they need to, but each person should be strong enough to do so. If we just take it when we're feeling held hostage, it only amplifies the power the other person has. It only increases the negative dynamic and entitlement routine.

Anybody who uses entitlement speeches is a psychological terrorist. Don't allow it! This is why safety nets are critical for everyone involved. I will not negotiate with anyone who manipulates a situation to their advantage over everyone else. I suggest you do the same.

A good way to know if any relationship or team dynamic is healthy is to think about how soldiers relate to members of their squad. They are trained to operate by the principle "no man left behind." Now imagine there's a group of soldiers running away from an enemy, and one guy gets injured and falls to the ground. Any teammate who doesn't go back is fighting for himself. He needs to be kicked out of the squad! You can't have that.

In any relationship you build—personal or business—everyone should know why they are in it and under what circumstances they should get out. This creates a no-hostage scenario where everyone is in the deal for the right reasons and they are empowered to be there.

Any deal is only as strong as its component parts and its participants.

SYSTEMS FOR REPLACEMENTS

One structure we have at POWERHOME SOLAR is we teach leaders to develop and empower their replacements. That protects the company, and it frees everyone to grow. Growth is an insurance policy, while stagnation is risky. Somebody who is growing can always find work either inside a company that values growth, like ours, or in new opportunities outside of it.

The **Never Be Held Hostage** principle ensures that if one person is out, the next person is up. It makes me think of the New England Patriots.

Quarterback Tom Brady is awesome, and his abilities within Coach Bill Belichick's system were a perfect match. Team success mostly relied on Brady's performance and Belichick's superb coaching, all supported by interchangeable supporting players—a next-man-up philosophy. At times, Brady had all-star talent, but he and Belichick largely won six Super Bowls over two decades because Brady committed to Belichick's system, they both got better with experience (they skilled up), and they stood in their values (winning).

When Brady outgrew the system, he left for the Tampa Bay Buccaneers, and the Patriots had no immediate answers for losing such a transcendent player. No team would. They were left in the dust while Brady moved on, and he took the Bucs to a Super Bowl victory.

No one wins anything alone—no one. And don't say boxers because the champs have epic trainers. Legendary boxing trainer Cus D'Amato was a star-maker for Mike Tyson. He not only molded Tyson to become the most amazing heavyweight fighter of all time, but he went beyond the role of coach and took Tyson into his home. He was a father figure.

Then there was Michael Jordan and Chicago Bulls coach Phil Jackson. Six NBA titles in eight years using Jackson's tried-and-true triangle offense. I could go on. Anyone who believes they can do everything themselves is operating from ego because they're scared and insecure. They're playing to avoid losing, rather to win, and that will hold you hostage every time.

Just having warm bodies in the building isn't enough.

At POWERHOME SOLAR, we're so serious about our high-performance culture that we fire a lot of people. We want people who are there because they are committed to the mission, to each other, and to their own personal success. It's why we constantly reshape the team to support those who are committed and let the others move on.

Think about opening a fridge where there is spoiled milk. That one carton stinks up the whole fridge! That's what happens in a team with low performers. The people who are there just for the sake of the job, hanging on, collecting a paycheck, are stinking up the whole system.

In a room of one hundred people, I see a distribution of work ethic that looks like this:

CHART 2—WORK ETHIC DISTRIBUTION

This chart illustrates a big truth in business and building teams. As a leader you want to nurture the top 20 percent that outrun everybody else. Seek those people. And if you're doing a count and you can't nominate enough people to be in the top 20 percent yet, then it is time to make some changes. Make room for new blood, and replace the ones on the bottom.

THE HARSH TRUTH: NATURE FIGURED IT OUT FOR US

Twenty percent of those people in almost any company are working their asses off. They're all in. They believe in the culture. They are keepers. They probably don't have a shelf life.

Sixty percent are putting in decent effort, their version of working hard. It's a little bit more than a job. They're earning what they get. They're not where the ass-kickers are, but it's good enough to get the job done. It's a fair transaction. Shelf life is possible.

Twenty percent are the laggards. Floating at the bottom, this group is slowing everyone else down, making excuses, pointing fingers, and not taking ownership.

The harsh reality is that you must constantly and quickly cut the bottom 20 percent and replace them—hopefully with more ass-kickers. Nature has figured it out. The herd is strong when the weakest fall away and there's room for new herd members. Cull your herd. It will keep your company strong.

SYSTEMS OF GROWTH AND OPPORTUNITY

As Jay Samit, the former Independent Vice Chairman of Deloitte and a guest I interviewed on my podcast in March 2021, would say, "You have to future-proof you." Samit also wrote a book called *Future-Proofing You: Twelve Truths for Creating Opportunity, Maximizing Wealth, and Controlling Your Destiny in An Uncertain World.*

"I got to visit Hearst Castle when I was kid. Any guy that can have polar bears and zebras, that's living," Samit joked on the day we sat down for our chat. That is gold. Imagine having such control of your life that no one could stop you.

Samit says approaching life with a growth mindset is one way to future-proof in this way—though maybe not to the extent of having zoo animals for pets. You want to stay open and optimistic. Every day when Samit wakes up, he tells himself, *Today can be better than yesterday, and I have the power to make it so.* Samit also told me as corny as that may seem, this phrase lights up synaptic nerves in your brain and opens you to opportunity.

The key component is this:

"I have the power to make it so."

If you tell yourself every day that you have the power to make it so, it's one simple way to think ahead and remain in control.

You have the power to make it so.

We all do.

To harness this, put a very simple process in place. Always seek opportunity. Approach each day with curiosity. How can I make this better? Where can I optimize? Who can I call on? Who has the knowledge I need, and how can I pull on that? What actions can I take that will shake things up, make it all feel new, and bring the unexpected?

Opportunity does not arrive from out of the clear blue sky. Opportunity is nurtured and created through new actions and reinvented old actions applied newly. Opportunity comes from discarding waste and bloat through optimization and making space for something new. Bring a willingness to change, reinvent, and optimize.

SKILL UP: GROW AND EXPAND YOURSELF

Are you focused on your personal growth? Do you have a system in place for it?

No matter how much of an A player you are on a team or in a partnership, you are responsible to keep growing—to skill up and build equity in you. This means business skills too.

Growth-minded performers don't get their futures handed to them by others. They make their own choices to stay where they are or move on to new opportunities. They decide whether they get held hostage or not.

Your next year should be better than the year before and the year before that. You should be getting healthier, wealthier, and wiser. Doing this requires effort. For me, it requires going to the gym and lifting weights. It means I must talk to better business leaders. I must listen to my team and learn where I need to improve. I see my therapist to talk out my issues and work on myself. I know if I don't do these things, I'll get lazy about my growth and put myself at risk of stagnation.

When I interviewed JeVon McCormick, CEO of Scribe Media, for my podcast, I was impressed by his skill-up attitude. "If I work one hundred times harder than you, my attitude is, I'm also one hundred times better than you." *Yes!* I thought. "Mindset, choices, and hard work equals success," he said.

Bam!

JeVon had a seriously tough upbringing. His father was a drug-dealing pimp, and his mom was an orphaned single mother on welfare. He was raised in the slums of Dayton, Ohio, where he suffered incredible abuse and racism. "I remember saying to myself one time in between beatings that I'm never going to be in a position in life where I don't know what to do."

He scrubbed toilets to work his way to better opportunities. He eventually became the president of two multimillion-dollar companies and is now the CEO of Scribe Media.

No one is perfect. I am certainly not. I have experienced both failures and successes, and I don't take either for granted. I learn from the failures and I celebrate the successes.

In 2015, with POWERHOME SOLAR, when we lost all that money because of a few sales guys and a misguided shortcut, I was held hostage. I didn't have the skills to run the sales operations anymore. I didn't know how to go out and sell our products anymore because I had spent my time away from the on-the-ground selling work.

After we let them go, we struggled. We lost money. We got close to shutting down. Before we did, I fired about 80 percent of the company. You read that right: 80 percent. I started over, and I grew the business back, starting from the bottom up.

Once we gained some traction, we started to flourish a little bit. In the second half of 2016, I brought Kevin back. He'd been working elsewhere because we couldn't pay him. He handled the marketing while I handled sales and operations, and it finally took off.

Looking back, I certainly learned the importance of building a growth-minded team that believes in the mission as much as I do. It's how we stay at the top of the industry and the top of our roles and win in all other areas of our lives.

I also learned that my lack of dedication could easily make me a victim. But in the end, I was held hostage by no one. And that's a magical place to be.

STAND UP FOR YOURSELF

The **Never Be Held Hostage** principle can sometimes be leveraged by standing up for what you believe in.

Long before the COVID-19 pandemic, when hand sanitizer wasn't cool, my wife was a germaphobe. As our relationship evolved and we got married, there were times when my parents would visit and get irritated by her requests: "Hey, you've got to take your shoes off when you come in the house," "Wash your hands," "Put sanitizer on before you touch the baby."

"What do you mean? It's not a big deal," my parents often said. You could see how they interpreted it: *Oh, we're dirty?* There was no ill intent, but they took it that way.

At the same time, they would criticize our parenting methods, right down to the formula we were feeding our babies. I don't blame my parents for what they did. They didn't know any better.

And now that I am a grandfather, I get that way too and constantly reel myself in.

I tried for years to make everybody happy. I understood how my parents felt and wanted their approval, so I tried to keep the peace. But in all honesty, I didn't accept responsibility that my kids and my wife were my primary commitment until about the age of thirty.

So when my parents fought with Liz and complained to me, I'd go to Liz and tell her she needed to change. Then she'd get mad at me for not defending her, and I would then go back and confront my parents.

Eventually I got fed up. I finally stood up to my parents. It was our rules and our house. I finally supported Liz and my family.

My parents were holding me (and us) hostage. I was compromising my values to keep them happy, but in the middle of it all, I was never happy. I had made myself into a victim.

One day Liz and my mom had a tiff. Liz was pregnant with our fourth baby at the time. I was in Nevada on a business trip when I got a call from her. She was crazy upset.

"Your mom started screaming at me, and I lost it," she said. "She shoulder-checked me." It wasn't violent, but it wasn't cool. It set Liz off. It set me off too.

I finally put my foot down, and I set boundaries. I said to my mom, "Just because we're blood related doesn't entitle you to anything.

A relationship goes both ways. It requires give and take from both parties. It is not one-sided. It is not a dictatorship."

"We're done," I told my parents that day. "If you are going to keep disregarding my wife's rules in our house, we're done. You're not going to be able to see our son be born."

It was an unfortunate circumstance for everyone, but it had to happen for change to take. After this day, there was a rift in our family that lasted for years. My parents didn't see my son until he was almost one. But slowly (and miraculously), and with some therapy and work, both sides came around.

The beauty of it is our relationships got stronger. Each party tried to understand the other side. Liz and my mom started to respect one another. And as the years have gone by, there's more respect today than there's ever been.

Liz and I also became better parents. We created a safety net around our family circle. Because of the rift, I sought new ways to be a better man too.

For the first time ever, faith became an important part of my life. I never went to church as a kid, but Liz did. "We need church in our life," she said. She saw it as a way for me to move through the struggles I was having with my parents. She also recognized it as a structure to help the family develop healthy habits, focus on our own growth journeys, and build toward a positive future.

It took us a while to find a church we liked. We tried everything— you name it, even Mormon and Catholic churches. Eventually we fell in love with one Baptist church. There I met these dads and husbands who showed me the type of man I wanted to be.

I re-proposed to my wife because she'd only ever had a shotgun wedding. "Marry me again," I said to her one night. Soon after we brought everyone together for a big flashy wedding.

It was 2011 when we remarried. And the night before, the entire family was baptized together. My parents also came, which was the start of building a new relationship. They still didn't come to the wedding, which was a shame, but slowly we all came back together.

Today, we have a healthy relationship. We have all changed completely. To get here, we needed to go through what we did. But I had to put my foot down. I had to take away their power for them to become humbler and more respectful. They are fantastic grandparents to my kids today.

You always must ask yourself what is most important and protect that first. When you refuse to compromise your values and you act from that place, you're applying the **Never Be Held Hostage** principle.

In learning to not be a hostage, I had to learn and put into practice five critical things:

1. **Don't be intimidated by people more educated than you.** In starting my first business, I was twenty-five years old, and I had to learn how to lead people who were ten or more years older than me and had gone to college. That was intimidating

at first. But you learn that it is you they are seeking answers from, and you need to be that person for them. You must learn what it takes to handle that role.

2. **Don't be afraid to let go.** When you build something from the ground up and know it better than anyone else, it's hard to see inefficiency happen and not want to step in and fix it right away. But I learned it's far more important to give people that opportunity and let them either sink or swim. Letting go is so hard, but it is truly what I needed to learn to take our business to the next level.

3. **Don't ever talk yourself out of saying, "Why not us?"** We have a goal at POWERHOME SOLAR, which is to be the biggest and best solar company in America. Some might say, "How can that happen when the guy leading the company was a high school dropout who also had his first child in his teens?" Thing is, there's never a cap on what you can accomplish. But you must put in the work. You must take the stairs. There is no elevator to success. You've gotta grind; you have to want it more than the person next to you. Look at where we're at now—tracking for $350 million in revenue this year. I'm just as hungry to keep climbing as I was when I first started, and our team is too.

4. **You can't always be the good guy in business.** There's always going to be a need to keep people in line in your business, and sometimes that means having frank discussions with people about performance. I never wanted to be that guy, but it's important to have a voice like that who can hold people accountable when it's needed.

5. **Hire and build with smarter people in different areas that needed to grow.** For me, one of those was adding a CFO who was able to take our financials to the next level

and keep a tighter rein on expenses and operations. We now have an accounting team of 7.5 people that is executing at an extremely high level, and they've done great work through better automated processes and tools. Also, even in building my *True Underdog* podcast, we hired a team that can take my burgeoning show to another level.

It takes courage, and it might take time. When you apply this principle, don't expect overnight success. Sometimes it will get uglier before it gets better. Just put your head down and grind it out from that place; keep operating from your core beliefs, and trust yourself. You will always get what you want if you stand firm in what you believe in.

CHAPTER CHALLENGE

NEVER BE HELD HOSTAGE

Take reflection time to think about your current situation. Use this section to analyze what is working in your business (and life) and what is holding you back. Go through this series of questions, and try to see as many options as you can in any situation. Get creative, and don't limit your thinking when answering the questions below. Then rip this page out of the book and hang it up somewhere you will see it every day—a bathroom mirror, your refrigerator, or the side of your computer monitor. The location doesn't matter, only that you see it every day. To change your underdog story, you must never be held hostage or limit your options for resetting what is not working. Reminding yourself to think differently, systemize, skill up, and stand up for yourself will push you further down the path as you learn to own your power.

1. Analyze your company's power structure. Who is in control?

....

....

2. Do any employees have too much power? **Circle one.**

Yes / No

3. What is at risk if those employees stop producing or leave?

....

....

....

....

4. What safety nets can you build that protect you and your business?

....

....

....

....

5. What skills do you need to strengthen?

....

....

....

....

6. What values are you compromising in the current situation?

....

CHAPTER FOUR

PRINCIPLE #4—SCARED MONEY DON'T MAKE MONEY

You can play it safe in life or play full out.

I've done both.

I played it safe for a long time. Then one day, when I had to risk everything, I won more than I ever had before. I became unstoppable. The level of risk determines the level of the reward, and there was nothing I couldn't achieve because I bet it all.

It wasn't because of what I bet but because my attitude changed. Losing wasn't an option.

That decision happened while my own family and I were on a trip to Disneyland in December 2015. Christmas was around the corner, so it was purely family time. I was trying to enjoy myself, but I couldn't relax. I was stressed about the company, our money, and our future.

At one point in the day, while the kids were on a ride, Liz and I sat down at a red picnic table nearby. We were both sweating profusely, licking ice cream cones, and waiting for the kids to finish.

"We're going to have to shut the doors," I said to Liz. "It's the first time I'm ever going to fail. I can't get this to work." I was talking about POWERHOME SOLAR. For a year, we'd been trying to get the business into profitability and just couldn't make it happen.

She looked at me but didn't say anything.

"Kevin thinks so too," I added. Kevin was by my side again for this venture. Like I said, he's my business ride or die.

Again, Liz didn't say much. The kids came back jacked full of adrenaline and talking a mile a minute, so we put the conversation on hold until later that night when we were alone in our hotel room.

I did have a solution to keep the doors open. I knew Liz wasn't going to be happy, but it was what we had to do.

At the end of my first year with POWERHOME SOLAR, the company was losing money and I had to consider shutting the doors. Cash flow was a real problem because we weren't getting paid until after projects were installed, and that was tough. I felt like the shot clock was running out, and I just needed more time. I had to talk my wife into listing our lake house for sale because we had built some equity, and we could go and buy a smaller house with cash and not have any bills. We were at that point. I've been defeated before, but I've never quit. What do I do? I was struggling with it. I was tearing up. My wife said, "You need to pray about it. Figure it out. I trust you. I have faith. You always come out on top. You always find a way."

With that, I made the decision to go all in. It was a huge risk, especially when my life savings were gone from my two prior businesses, but I love betting on myself.

"We are going to sell the lake house," I said.

Liz gave me the stink eye. But neither of us came up with a better idea. So that's what we did. We sold the lake house, and I stuck the money from the sale back into the business.

Let me pause for a moment here to tell you just how soul sucking it was to sell the lake house. We loved that property. The day we bought it was a dream, and so was pretty much every day that we lived there. The kitchen and living room were an open concept with a wall of windows. Our morning coffee conversations revolved around routine check-ins on mallard ducks. Our lakeview was peppered with speedboats that frequently motored by. In the summer months, smiling kids in tubes would whip from one end of our view to the other. Some of those kids were our own.

Scared Money Don't Make Money means you plan and go all in. Throw away the safety net. Take out all the excuses with the trash, and go balls to the wall all out, like your life depends on it, because it does. Bet it all.

There is no other way to live. Bet it all on yourself.

At that time, we needed to go all in. Everything we had from that point on was going into the business.

Before that moment, I always thought I was playing big, but really, I was playing it safe. I'd had two successful businesses up to this point. I'd become more successful than a lot of people, but still, I was playing it safe.

INVEST IN YOURSELF

When I opened my first successful business, it was in home security back in 2005. I did it with a dribble of money in my meager 401(k)—about $10,000—and a bankruptcy behind me from a previous bad business deal. Remember, I kept working at Bell Atlantic Verizon when I launched it because Liz was pregnant, and we needed the benefits.

I figured home security was a good business to get into because I had sold it over the phone while I was in high school. At Bell Atlantic, I was one of their top account managers, selling PDAs and BlackBerries. I was making great money, and Liz didn't need to work. But I felt handcuffed. I couldn't grow. I was also bored and felt I deserved more.

At Bell Atlantic, I wasn't getting promoted because of my age. So while my manager was one of the best mentors I ever had, he had limited ability to help me. People with high school educations had to be in a position fifteen years before he could move them to the next level. I had only been there two years. I was the top performer, but I was still a kid. I hadn't been there long enough for him to promote me.

So I took my 401(k) money and used it to hire a flyer team. My dad had also received a dismal retirement package from AT&T, so I paid him a bit of cash to drive a bunch of minimum wage kids around to hang flyers on doors. Remember those?

FREE ALARM SYSTEM.
FREE GARAGE OPENER INSTALL.

Every night, I came home from my day job and made calls to sell home security systems. I also drove limos on weekends. My day job paycheck supported our basic living costs, and all the extra money I made was reinvested in the company.

I was grinding it out and building, slow and steady, but I was playing it safe.

When I finally made enough in the side business to cover our expenses and float some growth, I quit and left the corporate job behind. This business ran from 2005 to 2012. I kept failing and learning, failing, and learning.

After the bankruptcy in 2002, I had adopted a "buy it with cash" mindset. And I was cautious, so I moved slowly. I didn't want another big loss, so I wasn't willing to take another big risk. But sometimes you need to. I wasn't betting on myself yet.

Then in 2012, my company joined Power Home Technologies. That was a wild bet, a pivot. It may have seemed like a safe bet. But as I look back on it, it was a crab walk and a sideways move that may have come from playing it safe. We both got value from the merger. They had done $18 million that year in sales. So we worked out a deal. But the new entity meant I wasn't number one anymore. That was different for me. Still, we worked well together. By the time I sold it, we were doing $12 million a year in sales.

It is true that I often had a different vision on our approach in the new business. Not that mine was better—we just had different styles. My alarm company was more profitable on a percentage basis because I'd been in the trenches, and my partner Ben was much better at trusting people than I was. He was great at building relationships.

Again, joining Ben at Power Home Technologies was a safe bet. It was a pivot that worked. I got an employment contract and wasn't the sales leader. But we grew to $38 million in annual sales and went from 4 percent profit to 8 percent. As far as I could tell back then, we killed it.

We were growing, but internally, I felt handcuffed. I wanted to get into solar panels, and my partners weren't listening to what I was preaching. So I reached out to a competitor both of us knew, and they bought us out. Another pivot. My partners, Ben and Eric, stayed on as employees, and Kevin and I left to go do solar.

The plan was for Ben and Eric to become partners in solar. But we had a falling out and fundamental disagreement at a Christmas party. The deal was dead. They were going to remain in the security business. The mutual agreement was to go our own ways.

The first day of 2015 was my official first day away from Power Home Technologies and the day I became CEO of POWERHOME SOLAR. This time, I had no reserve, no safety net, no day job paying the bills. Sure, our exit payout was $1.5 million. It was $500,000 upfront and the rest over the next two years. I had no money for the new solar business, and I didn't know much about the industry yet either.

Except for a telemarketing business that we owned and Kevin ran that earned us a small paycheck, we were screwed. Months went by, and POWERHOME SOLAR wasn't panning out. Until I risked everything.

We kept losing money. I had put all the money from the sale of Power Home Technologies into POWERHOME SOLAR. Neither Kevin nor I took a paycheck for twenty-two months. When we sold the lake house in 2016, no one was happy about it. Not me. Not Liz. Not the kids. But we did it anyway. I needed the money to put into POWERHOME SOLAR.

It's amazing what you can accomplish when you have no alternatives. I cleaned house of some company leaders who were not buying in, and I started running the sales department and training reps myself. I made deals, did all I could to turn things around, and got our team passionate about the direction we were headed. It started working, and the business started to grow. Through selling my house and getting some cash flow relief from vendors that started paying us a portion of deals upfront because of our performance, things started turning for the better. My first paycheck came eighteen months after starting the business. My rule in every company I've ever built, run, or been a part of is you pay your staff first, your vendors second, and yourself last. That made it easier to keep going, but it was still far from easy. A lot of entrepreneurs want to pay themselves first, and that's a mistake. You have to be humble.

We bought a much smaller house with cash—so there was no mortgage. The money left over was fire-hosed into the business. I activated my **Scared Money Don't Make Money** principle for the first time, before I really knew what it was all about.

I told my employees, "I sold my house so you can be paid, so you can be part of a movement, so we can all succeed together."

I shared my story, and they felt it.

It's not about being heard; it's about being felt. When you have passion, strong people will follow you anywhere.

If you can't bet on yourself with everything you've got, then nobody else will. No employees will join your team. No partners will invest in you. No customers will want to buy from you.

You can't expect somebody else to bet on you if you won't bet on you.

As you will learn soon in this chapter, this isn't only about a bet with dollars. You also must go all in with your skills and your confidence. You bring all your assets to the table every time in everything you do.

If you believe in something and want it bad enough, you must be willing to put it all on the line or it will never work. Dump all your savings into the business you want to build.

Dump your side gigs. Tell everyone what your mission is, and speak boldly about it. People won't want to be a part of what you're doing unless you're fully invested.

By the end of 2016, we had over $14 million in sales. That was five times more than we'd sold in 2015. We even started to get a paycheck in November of 2016.

The **Scared Money Don't Make Money** principle is about betting on yourself.

Put it all on the line. Make it known. Go all in. And then get it done.

SUCCESS IS NOT EARNED; IT'S CLAIMED

The **Scared Money Don't Make Money** principle is not limited to business or financing a business. It can be about money, like when I cashed in my lake house for the business. But sometimes, it just means to seize the moment by going all in on a situation or a person.

For some people, **Scared Money Don't Make Money** might look like quitting freelance gigs to have the time and freedom to go all in with a company. Or it might be to pivot fully and go back to school to get a PhD. Betting on yourself could also mean putting aside doubts and fears and committing to a relationship by proposing to the person you want to be with for the rest of your life.

It's about committing to yourself and then following through with bold action, even if you're scared. You face your fears, and you act anyway. And usually, you'll find after the first few actions that the fear diminishes or disappears completely.

Scared Money Don't Make Money is what Obama, Bush, and Clinton did when they took the first COVID-19 vaccine injections to demonstrate to the American people to be courageous and do it too. They put their own health on the line so others would follow their lead. They were betting big.

It's not easy or comfortable to bet this big. But here's the truth about being uncomfortable: your fears are in your head only. It's you that holds you back. Committing to yourself and going all in is embracing the fear to a point that it is inactivated, and it doesn't own you.

When I sold the lake house, I was terrified, but once I committed and followed through, I switched gears. I went into playoff game mode. I refused to fail, and because I had that mindset, I had energy. I woke up with a mission. I was clear on my purpose. Everything was about winning from that point on. Every little move I made became critical.

Scared Money Don't Make Money is also about sharing your mission with everyone around you. It is commitment with accountability. When you are bold, deliberate, and passionate, people are inspired by you. They build their own missions. They get excited. The momentum builds. Playing big is way more fun.

If life was a poker game, **Scared Money Don't Make Money** would be like you had got pocket aces every time.

You bet on yourself by putting it on the line with action and follow-through. Even when you're afraid, you move forward because you understand that success is not earned; it's claimed. You bet on the moment by using every minute to your advantage.

One day, I was chatting with John LeBlanc, who's a cohost of my podcast, *True Underdog*, and he said to me, "You know the difference between a buffalo and a cow, don't you?"

I didn't know where he was going with it. "No idea," I said.

"When there's a storm coming, the cow runs from the storm," he said. "But when a buffalo sees a storm, it runs toward it to get through it faster."

That's kind of genius.

We've all been intimidated and scared of what's in front of us. But if you invoke the buffalo mentality to seize the moment and take on your fear, you can confront it and deal with it faster.

Some people watch life happen, while others make it happen. Don't be a watcher, like a cow shivering under a tree as the storm brews. Bet on yourself to be something more than that. Take action. Make something happen.

Run toward the fear; brace yourself, and merge with your moment.

When you experience that instinct to fight or flee from a fear, pause to remember why you're betting on yourself:

- What am I here to achieve?
- Am I a cow or a buffalo?
- What are my options?

COVID-19 AND THE BUFFALO

During the worst year most businesses have experienced in recent times—I'm talking about COVID-19, of course—my team became buffalos.

My executive team and I were taking calls six, seven, or eight hours a day. We were on with the Centers for Disease Control, the health department, and corporate lawyers all day every day for weeks. The country shut down, but our business was essential.

The day after GM executives lowered their pay and it made headlines, I had a conference call with our executives to decide if we were going to stay open. Most of the team said we should furlough and shut down. "No, we're not going to do that. We're not closing," I said. It got heated.

I told them we weren't closing because Lucy, who was in the call center and was a single mom, needed to buy formula and diapers. And, Mike, who was an installer and the only provider for his house had rent to pay. Jim was close to retirement and needed every penny he could earn. I put my foot down. I had another plan.

"We're all going to go off payroll until further notice," I said, which created more heat. "I don't give a shit. If we're not willing to give back to our team to make sure we stay open, we shouldn't be on this call anyway."

Everyone agreed. Together at that moment, we all switched from cow to buffalo mode. We asked ourselves the critical questions to inform our strategy. Then everyone put on their big-boy pants.

We told the team the next day. We told them that we were not staying open for profits; we were staying open for them. We could not get any help from the government. We had 750 employees at the time. We were too big.

We also called our vendors. We pushed all payments down a few months, and we told them our story. I drove my ass to the Troy, Michigan, office, where I recorded a live video with a face mask to reassure our team that we were going to get through this together. We typed up a motivational email that went out to the company. It said:

Dear Team,

Fear is not for us to dictate. Everybody's situation is completely different. Some of you are very scared and you want to stay home, and that's okay. We will pay you your vacation time and your PTO time until it's gone, and when you go inactive, you'll keep your benefits.

Some of you have to have a paycheck. We're going to make it as safe as possible for each and every one of you to come into work. As long as customers are willing to buy, we're going to stay open and are willing to let you work and make money.

Sincerely,

Jayson

This is what being a buffalo looks like in action. It's a full-on mental state that encompasses the qualities of bravery, strength, and tenacity. Buffalos don't give up. They plow forward. They merge with difficult weather. They take on dangerous conditions. They charge head on into the hunters and elements that try to take them down. They demonstrate courage, endurance, and determination.

Each buffalo sacrifices itself to protect the herd, which also happened at POWERHOME SOLAR. When the leadership team shared that they would not take a salary, it became infectious. A group of thirty employees offered to withhold a portion of their salaries to help their colleagues and allow the company to stay open.

Anyone can embrace the qualities of the buffalo. All it takes is practice. The best way to bet on yourself is to take bold action. Be courageous.

Be the buffalo and run toward fear. Confront it head on. Or better yet, be the storm. Maybe you should be the one the cows are running from. Hell yeah!

BET ON THE MOMENT: MAXIMIZE EVERY OPPORTUNITY

Fear is the great destroyer of success. It annihilates opportunity before it has a chance to take hold and deliver you to where you need to go. Your management of fear is key to both your personal and business success. Strangle it as it strikes, and you have a chance. Fail to confront it, and you'll miss out on amazing and sometimes life-changing opportunities. It will take you down before you even start.

Massively successful entrepreneurs are living proof that success is about taking uncalculated risks. Future-proofing your business against things like COVID-19 means you're going to take some risks—and screw up along the way. Knowing how to fail quick, pivot, and try again is the key. It's how ideas become billion-dollar businesses.

One of my favorite business stories is about the Dollar Shave Club. The founder, Michal Dubin, had this crazy idea that the emerging trend of subscription boxes would help his company not just grow but also thrive. He had just entered a new market with an emerging revenue model, which is always risky.

Dollar Shave Club supplies men with shaving equipment. It first emerged in 2012, when the market was already dominated by existing brands. According to *Entrepreneur*, Gillette had a 72 percent market share. This dominance is what Dollar Shave Club was up against, but Michael Dubin didn't let the fear of that huge number deter him. Dubin believed that customers would prefer to get their complete shaving essentials delivered rather than venturing to the store. Right or wrong, he made his own map and started driving toward making Dollar Shave Club the answer to this problem.

The deck was stacked against Dubin. He went all in. He bet on himself.

Dollar Shave Club grew to be the top online razor company by 2016 with 51 percent of the market. Gillette launched its own online shaving subscription box but never could compare to the innovative marketing techniques employed by Dollar Shave Club. It is still the online industry leader.

By taking bold action and not giving into fear, the creators of Dollar Shave Club enjoyed a company sale of $1 billion. Not a bad reason to be the buffalo.

BIGGER OPPORTUNITIES EQUAL BIGGER FEAR. IT DOESN'T MATTER.

Let me tell you a story about the day I met President Trump. It was September 2020, and COVID-19 was raging across the US. It was only maybe five days before Trump himself got the disease.

I'd been invited to participate in a roundtable meeting of energy executives at the Trump International Hotel in Washington, DC, a few blocks from the White House. There were twenty-one of us there to talk about the future of energy.

First there was a pre-event cocktail reception with maybe eighty people in a grand reception room that was gold and white and dripping with chandeliers. The building was formerly a grand post office when it was first built in 1899, but Donald Trump turned it into a luxury hotel in 2016.

So I was in this amazing grand room where I knew no one. I'd been introduced by email to Ronna Romney McDaniel, the Republican National Congress Chair, prior to the event. But I didn't see her in the room yet.

I started chatting with a very nice lady who introduced herself as Gene. She was a billionaire. Then another lady came over. I was mingling with billionaires. These people came from stupid money. I mean, they were talking about their jets and helicopters.

Usually, I can carry my own. I don't get intimidated. But most of these people were in oil. They were older than me by at least a decade, maybe two or three. And they were all dolled up in top-notch suits, with the women all elegant, decorated in fancy jewelry. I'll be honest: I was not feeling confident. So I excused myself and found the washroom.

I splashed water on my face and looked at myself in the mirror. The blond guy looking back at me was tense. But I'd seen the look before on myself.

When I first started my company, I was incredibly insecure. All these smart people working for me, and I was supposed to know how to run the operation? That was then, and I got over it.

Most people run when they get scared. Still, in the bathroom that day at Trump International, I wasn't having it. *Get off your ass, and stop being a wuss,* I barked at myself. *Time to step up. I've got this,* I told my reflection.

I walked out of there determined to own the room. I rolled back into the ballroom, back among the oil billionaires. And I elbow-rubbed. I peacocked and talked them all up. Handed out my card. Let them know that I love me some me. And they all started to love me too.

At the best of times, I don't fit in. I have always been an outlier. Today was no different. I was wearing red tennis shoes, a t-shirt, jeans, and a $5,000 custom jacket. I never want to be like anyone else.

Bam!

I gave Gene a high five. She loved the shoes and wanted a picture. Click. We chatted, and she laid out for me how it was going to go with Trump. "He only answers like four or five questions. You might not get a chance because there are twenty-one of you," she explained.

"I'm a bull. I'll get to ask the question," I tell her.

"I'm just saying you might not be able to."

I smiled. *I've got this.*

At the roundtable, there were twenty-five seats, twenty-one for the guests and four for his staff. Trump came in and sat at the end table where there was no one next to him. His nameplate said, "President of the United States." Pretty wild.

Still, I was in the moment, not letting it overtake me. That's key. When you're in moments like this, you can't let the moment control you. If the moment gets bigger than you, you're done. That wave's going to hit you hard, and you're going to drown.

You know how the greats win the Super Bowl or the World Series? They control the moment. They own it. The same on free throws that win NBA championships. That's how wars are won too. You must be in the moment and have full control.

After Trump sat down, a guy in the hotel business lobbed the first question. His properties had mortgage issues. Trump summoned his Chief of Staff, Mark Meadows. "Call the banks. Let's help this guy out," Trump told Meadows.

"Okay, next question," said POTUS.

Most of the people there were just excited to be at the table. For me, being at the table wasn't enough. Being at the table is elementary. Doing something at the table is making a difference. The game-changer is swallowing your fear and insecurity and getting into the conversation—being someone at the table who matters.

My agenda was simple. I needed to make an impact, to ensure that every time this guy thought of solar, he thought of me and my company. He needed to remember me forever. That was important to me.

It was my turn. "Mr. President!" I automatically spoke up. I was not spectating today.

"Yes?" said Trump.

"Jayson Waller, POWERHOME SOLAR—" That's as far as I got.

"Hold on. POWERHOME SOLAR. You do solar for residential?" he asked.

"Yes, Mr. President. I do."

He replied, "Okay. So how do you feel about the China tariffs that we put in place a few years ago? Did it help your business?"

"It did," I told him.

"Just so you know, China was dumping their panels in here for a third of the cost. And we couldn't get any American-made panel companies to manufacture here. How many now? Like five or seven different companies?" he asked.

"Yeah. That's where we get our panels," I said.

He said, "Good, good. Well, I'm glad to help the business. So everybody understands that change, that we added jobs here. Go ahead."

So I said, "Well, Mr. President, the perception in our business is that solar is Democratic. You see, that is a problem for us. The strange reality is 70 percent of our customers are Republican. They are the landowners, and they want to own their own power source and not be held hostage by a utility."

I told him we bought American since now there was an American supply of panels. We employed 1,700 people. And we were in twenty-two markets across the country. Our run rate was on pace to do $700 million under the Trump administration.

He was impressed. We bantered back and forth for a total of twelve minutes. By the end of the chat, I asked him to spread the word and tell people that solar was an American thing. "It's not a political thing. It's not Republican or Democrat. It's American."

"You've got it," he said.

I know I made an impression. In fact, in the next debate he said he liked American solar.

You know what got me to own the moment? Me. I gave myself

a pep talk in the bathroom. A little self-talk now and again is never bad. You must run the show when it comes to the voice in your head.

And then when I walked back into that room, I acted before I was comfortable. I straightened my shoulders and moved my body around the room with swagger. I stood near key people and chatted them up. I spoke up and raised my hand to get the attention of the president. Before my brain could register what I was doing, I was taking powerful actions.

Being too scared to do something is a senseless excuse. You can be scared and act anyway. You're no different than me. You can do the same anytime.

CHAPTER CHALLENGE

SCARED MONEY DON'T MAKE MONEY

Take reflection time to think about your comfort level with being bold and taking risks. Use this section to think about the money you are leaving on the table because you are too timid or too stuck in the story you've been telling yourself about what is possible. Go through this series of questions, and get a handle on how fear is helping or hurting you. Be honest with your answers. Then rip this page out of the book and hang it up somewhere you will see it every day—a bathroom mirror, your refrigerator, or the side of your computer monitor. The location doesn't matter, only that you see it every day. To change your underdog story, you can't give into fear or avoid risk. Learning to bet on yourself is how you get closer to success and living a life where you own your power.

1. Identify the areas where you are holding back.

   ....

   ....

   ....

   ....

2. What negatives is this creating in your business or personal life?

   ....

....

....

....

3. Would your business benefit more from a deeper commitment of your time or by putting more money into it? **Circle
   one.**

More time → More money

4. What difference could it make to your business or your personal life if you stopped being afraid to take a risk? **Describe
   it.**

....

....

....

....

Now is the time to develop a fear-fighting strategy and put it into
action. When you do, post your victory. Hold others accountable. Free the hostages. Use hashtags #OYPDontBeHeldHostage,
#OwnYourPower, or #JaysonWaller to celebrate your wins.

CHAPTER FIVE

PRINCIPLE #5—TURN FAILURE INTO FUEL

Bill Gates is a genius businessman and softspoken philanthropist who now runs a foundation that's dedicated to improving global health. He's a real stand-up citizen. But he's also publicly admitted he was an angry and difficult boss in his early days running Microsoft.

CNBC published an article about Gates in 2021, with the headline, "Bill Gates Says He Could Be as Tough on His Employees as Michael Jordan Was on His Teammates: 'I Certainly Wasn't a Sweetheart.'"

He was notorious for sending critical and sarcastic emails late at night. Apparently, he dropped the f-bomb more than you could count on two hands during most meetings. His former colleagues said they were always scrutinized.

Gates was a jerk—and many of his employees still liked him.

"You always knew what Bill thought about what you were doing," said one former teammate.

"The motivational force for programmers was to get Bill to like their product," another person said.

I read this article because my leadership team sent it to me. I wasn't surprised at the comparison. I can be very hard on people. And hard on myself. But when they made the comparison that day, I took a hard look at my leadership style.

Heading into 2021, I challenged myself to learn how to communicate more effectively. I told my wife. I told my kids. I told my executive team, "I want to communicate more effectively, which means I don't want to lose control as much as I do."

I have traits that are assets and weaknesses. Reality check moment: we all do. But you can't do better if you don't look at where you suck.

People think you relax a bit as you get older. Not this guy. I love to watch the people around me win, but because of this, I have high expectations and a very short temper. The many life challenges I've faced make my tolerance level for losing lower than most. I go from one to two to ten. There is no slow build-up when I communicate.

When I told everybody that I was going to learn to control myself more, it meant I wanted to learn to go one-two-breathe-three-four-five...then maybe I'd try for ten. The fact is, I am stronger when I don't blow up. A lack of self-control is a weakness that I've had to work on over time.

My tendency to jump on people comes from a good place. Maybe you have that character trait too. There is value to being a no-BS kind of guy. I always tell people to quit making excuses. When a member of my leadership tells me why we had a bad month in our business, I tell them to not make dumb excuses. People don't have to like me all the time. Part of being a great leader is being a coach.

Sometimes a little tough love is necessary. Sometimes people appreciate it later.

It's how we got to the promised land, trying to go public, and have been more profitable year after year.

But when I get upset and "blow," it's not the way to get the best out of the people around me.

It's because I want everyone to think like me. Sometimes I'm wrong. When I'm tough, I can push people away. I drop bombs. Sometimes I screw myself and my team over by being too pushy. To be successful—especially when it comes to my commitment to communicate better—I must be willing to examine my flaws.

That doesn't always feel good, but it's so valuable. Now when I hit a wall that used to make me explode, I seek help. I talk it through with business mentors, my wife, and my therapist. I have a council that I go to.

Failure is a signal for you to learn a new behavior and seek out people who are great at what you're not so you can course correct. As I've gotten better at handling failure, I've learned how to use it as fuel.

> **Success without failure is rare. You can live a risk-averse life, but it won't get you far. Failure is our ultimate education. Embrace it. Understand that it has nothing to do with how worthy you are. Treat failure as a performance metric. Take the emotion out of it. Fail. Learn. Recalibrate. Repeat.**

I make a lot of athlete analogies, I know, but again it's fitting here. Athletes are always practicing. They are always getting better. They fail. They evaluate. They change up their strategy, and they try again until they succeed. Always get better. AGB, remember? To get better, you must get cool with failure.

Failure is your partner. It's your friend. It's your fuel. Think of an area in life where you're very successful. How much did you fail to get where you are today? Most of what I've ever learned in life isn't because of education—it's because of trying, failing, and trying again.

To get better at failure you must learn to:

- Relate to failure as a performance metric and nothing else.
- Celebrate failure because it means you're playing a big game in life.
- Focus forward because grudges hold you back.

Consider this chapter your failure reconditioning. Welcome to boot camp. It's time to turn failure into fuel.

> **Don't be intimidated by people more educated than you. In starting my first business, I was twenty-five years old, and I had to learn how to lead people who were ten or more years older than me and had gone to college. That was intimidating at first. But you learn that it is you they are seeking answers from, and you need to be that person for them. You must learn what it takes to handle that role.**

FAILURE IS AN OPPORTUNITY

Many of us are conditioned to believe from childhood that if you fail, you've screwed up and you're a bad kid. But you need failure to get to success. To embrace failure, you must stop seeing it as an obstacle and start relating to it as a gift or an opportunity. If you don't fail, you can't get better at anything. When failure shows up, it's an opportunity to examine what happened, look for ways to avoid that hang-up next time, and put processes in place to turn it around, improve, and win.

If you're not failing, you're getting complacent.

The **Turn Failure into Fuel** principle reminds you to separate the failure from these negative emotions by seeing it as useful to getting to success. Failure is no more than a performance metric or a measurement of your progress.

How do we know when a football team loses a game? We look at the score. That score is a measurement of effort. The more points, the higher the score. If your team scores more points than the other team, you win. If you score less, you lose. The score is a performance metric.

What's funny about it all is that most people only remember your successes—not the failures that seemed so obvious to us at the time. People usually don't know the backstory of an achievement. They don't know the wounds, the sleepless nights, the loss of paychecks, or the loss of friends and family that it took to get there. Be like them! Keep your eyes on the achievement you're after.

IF YOU PLAY BIG, YOU WILL FAIL

When it comes to any goal you want to achieve, make sure you are always stretching a little more. That's the key to staying at the top of your game at anything. That means you *should* be failing. If not, you're not challenging yourself enough.

My seventeen-year-old daughter, Mackenzie, plays a lot of what's called travel softball. Basically, the team travels almost every weekend for tournaments, and the level of competition is intense. Since her birthday is at the very end of the year (she was almost a January baby, but Liz was induced, and she was born on New Year's Eve), she always had to play with teams with players who were a year or two older than her. Because she never played with kids her own age, she didn't have the physical ability, size, or strength to be the best player on a travel team.

It was hard for her. I also put her in a recreational softball league so she could build confidence, and on those pay-to-play teams, she was one of the best. On her travel team, she started at the bottom and worked her way to the middle.

But that's the beauty of it. The middle is the best spot. You're hungry to get to the top, but you're not at the bottom getting constantly replaced.

My daughter's age disadvantage made her better. Had she been born a day later, she could have been on a team where the competition was less intense, and she wouldn't have needed to try as much.

If you find yourself at the top, look for other people to stretch toward. Stay in the performance sweet spot by always setting higher personal KPIs (key performance indicators).

At POWERHOME, we track KPIs and evaluate roles and performance. When the numbers aren't where they need to be, we churn and burn (fire 20 percent of the staff). That's why we've grown straight up without flatlining. It's scary, but you won't get anywhere in life if you're not trying.

When someone is all in and doing everything they can to get better, I fight for them. Anyone in our organization who embraces feedback and criticism and demonstrates that they are open to learning has an indicator of future success. That mentality is to be respected.

If you're failing, it's a good thing. Just make sure you bounce back. It's not about you and your worth—it is a measurement of your performance and an indicator that you're growing.

THE BENEFITS OF FAILURE

I have played in the World Series of Poker four times. I even bought into the $50,000 high-stakes just to play with all the big boys—guys like Joe Cada and Daniel Negreanu. It was amazing. And I'm certainly no poker world champ.

My friends thought I was crazy to spend $50,000 to lose to world champions. But I wanted to experience the game at that level to see what it was like. I wasn't going to boo-hoo if I failed. Plus, there are only about one hundred people who play in the World Series of Poker $50,000 High Roller tournament, and they pay nineteen winners. I had a 19 percent chance of doubling my money or more. In the main event, there's a 10 percent chance of doubling your money, and you play against 6,000 people. The main event was eleven days long. So of course, I was willing to spend more and play with the big boys for a two-day tournament.

Losing would mean that I was not as great a player as them—and I knew that. I'd also learn what to do to get better, and I'd get to build relationships with them. I played with the best in the world, and I placed twenty-third. I didn't cash out, but I took two world pros out. That was enough for me.

I failed, but how many people can say they played the World Series of Poker with the best in the world and eliminated some pros along the way? If I was scared to fail, I wouldn't have gotten to do that.

The best way to look at failure is to shift your context around it. Failure isn't bad. It doesn't mean you're not a worthy person, so don't get personal about it. Failure is a performance metric that shows you where you fall in the pack and what you need to work on to get better. This mindset is how you can use failure to your advantage instead of letting it hold you back.

FOCUS FORWARD

When people can't let go of the past, I tell them, "Your eyes are in the front of the head, so focus forward."

What I mean by that is that it is a waste of time to suffer over what has happened in the past. When you focus on the past, you are not concentrating on the future. Said another way, you can't drive very fast if you are constantly looking in your mirrors. If you're not careful, you'll drive your ass off the road.

In the heat of the moment, I forget this little pearl of wisdom too. I must remind myself that being mad or overly focused on a loss in the past takes your energy away from the present. Deal with the situation; then move on.

If you have had a business failure, learn from it. Analyze. What factors influenced the failure? Identify decisions and actions that led you off track and learn from them so that they won't be repeated. If outside circumstances were a contributing factor, decide how you might have reduced their influence. Make this a learning experience, and use it to inform your decisions.

Recently, when I interviewed David Meltzer, my mentor, friend, and cohost on 2 *Minute Drill*, about how he started over when he hit rock bottom, what he said was powerful: "I told myself if I can look up, I can get up."

He said this to himself while lying in bed watching his cars being taken away as he was being moved out of his house. "I lay in bed, for the first time depressed, and what comes on the TV? *Rocky I*."

Rocky kept getting knocked down. Apollo Creed just kept slugging him. And David just watched. What did he watch Rocky do? He got back up. He gave David the strength to get back up too. If you can look up, you can get up. We all need this reminder sometimes.

One trick for thinking ahead is to avoid getting caught up in asking yourself why questions. They are past based. People get too caught up in the why. Why did this person hurt me? Why did this happen to me? Why did I mess up again? This type of thinking is looking back when the only answers you're going to get will come from you, the person who is mad about what happened. And trust me, those answers won't be good. It usually looks like: *Why did I fail? Because I suck.* Or *Why did they hurt me? Because they suck.*

Why questions are often useless. All they do is put you in a negative thought-loop with yourself.

Instead, engage curiosity with some forward-looking questions:

- I failed, which is a performance breakdown. What happened, and what do I need to do next time to do better?
- What am I committed to?
- What actions do I need to take to get closer to achieving the goal I'm committed to?

My wife and I both came from imperfect homes. Her dad was in prison, making her mom a single mom. Her mom was not a good mom. She rejected Liz time and time again. She never showed unconditional love. My parents were not highly educated, and at times, the way they spoke to each other wasn't healthy. They were abusive both physically and verbally to each other, as well as to me and my siblings. They tried the best they could. I could stay upset, but that'd be looking back and nursing a grudge. Instead, I can appreciate that they had an upbringing and life that shaped them into the people they became. And that influenced me.

When it came to my kids, my wife and I had to fail and learn and fail again as parents. Hannah, my twenty-two-year-old, didn't get my best self, and probably not my wife's best self either.

If we had gotten a report card for our parenting, we were possibly a C with Hannah. With my seventeen-year-old, Mackenzie, we might have reached a C+. Then, with my thirteen-year-old, Londyn, we were probably at a solid B. I hope that Christian, my ten-year-old son, is getting a B+ or better. If not, we'll just continue learning and failing like we always have.

To be a better dad and mom, we have had to move on from the past. We are committed to being the best damn parents we can be, no matter what our upbringing was. We evolved. We had to fail, assess, and remind ourselves of what we were committed to so we could take new actions. And that makes us much better than if we'd spent all our time looking back. You can do the same.

CHAPTER CHALLENGE

TURN FAILURE INTO FUEL

Take reflection time to think about the times that you have utterly failed in life. Use this section to dissect those moments when failure overtook you. Go through this series of questions, and look at how failure is working for you. Be honest with your answers. Then rip this page out of the book and hang it up somewhere you will see it every day—a bathroom mirror, your refrigerator, or the side of your computer monitor. The location doesn't matter, only that you see it every day. To change your underdog story, you must use failure as a success tool, not a mark of shame. It's a big trick on how to own your power.

1. What are the last five failures you experienced in business?

....

....

....

....

....

2. What did those five failures teach you? **Describe it.**

....

....

....

....

....

Now is the time to face your failures, learn from them, and use them to make your next move. When you do, post your victory. Hold others accountable. Celebrate failure. Use hashtags #OYP-FailureIsGood, #OwnYourPower, or #JaysonWaller to celebrate your wins.

CHAPTER SIX

PRINCIPLE #6—LOVE YOUR HATERS

Everyone has people who don't like them. It doesn't matter what your station in life is. But you can't let the haters stop you. Instead, embrace what they say, and use it as fuel. The best way to show the haters not to hate is to stay in your lane and succeed. When you win, they'll question their views. They might even join your team. So don't get caught up in negativity. Focus on your own success, and teach everyone around you to do the same.

In Chapter Four, I told you that when Kevin and I started POW-ERHOME SOLAR, we had plans to have our former partners at Power Home Technologies, Ben, and Eric, join us. But we had a falling out. Our deal didn't go through. They didn't believe in solar.

"We don't want anything to do with solar," Ben said. "We're going to stay with home security. Have fun."

The falling out happened at the end of December 2014. Then, in February 2015, we were all supposed to attend a trade show event in Mexico called MONI X. It's an annual gathering for the top alarm dealers that have broken sales records. It's paid for by Monitronics, which is a national security company that provides top-rated monitoring services and installations. The four of us had been in their dealer program before the split.

"We don't need to go to that," Kevin said.

"No, we won the trip. We should go," I told him.

I called Monitronics, and we got the okay because we were part of a home security company when we won, even though we'd moved on to solar. But we were torn. Everyone there would still be in home security.

We chose to go. But we felt insecure because we were on our way out of the business. Everyone else there ran alarm companies, and we had a brand-new solar company with five employees and no history or credentials.

So there we were with our peers who we'd competed with. We

had great relationships with many of them. With a few others, the relationships weren't so good. Ben and Eric were there too. It was awkward.

Meanwhile, Kevin and I were excited. We were passionate about solar. We believed in it. We chatted with our peers and explained our next chapter in life. Their reactions reminded me of when I opened my first business. No one believed I'd succeed. Some of them were downright jerks: "Bad idea. That won't work." Most of them didn't badmouth us to our faces, but they were passive-aggressive about what they thought, which was worse.

The haters deflated our enthusiasm for the new business. And they made us feel less-than.

I'm sure it's happened to you at some point. You share an idea you're excited about with a friend, family member, or business associate. And they kill it right then and there: "I hope it works well for you. But, um, I wouldn't do that."

The people who love us most can be our worst critics. But I had become an adult. I had already had success, running two profitable multimillion-dollar businesses, and I'd learned how to use haters as fuel to make me hungrier.

The home security crowd didn't get our vision. But I could see the future. It was like I saw the world in UltraHD, and they saw only fuzzy black and white. We left Mexico at the end of that trip a little bothered. But we channeled the pain as motivation to win in solar. I wanted to win even more.

The best way to prove to the haters who you are and who they can be is to show them. Haters can be used as a motivator to get into action. Use them to push yourself harder. Don't operate from the mentality that you are better than them, but show them what you are made of. Show them what could be possible for them if they dropped the mockery and focused on themselves.

In other words, the way to deal with haters is to focus on your own success.

SQUASH HATE BY EMBRACING IT

I had lots of haters before I was successful.

They were the kids who judged me in high school. They'd harass me about aspects of my life I couldn't control, like how much money my parents made. They were my in-laws in the early days who didn't think I was good enough for Liz because I lived in a trailer park. Some of my family doubted me when I started my first business too. A lot of people didn't believe in my alarm business. They thought it was a joke, and they mocked me.

I still have haters, even after building three successful businesses, becoming a husband and father who takes care of his family, and starting a solar movement to improve the world. Maybe I have more haters than ever. Nothing I do will get rid of them. Nothing you do will get rid of yours.

Everyone has haters. It doesn't matter where you are in life.

- Are you failing in life? You have haters!

- Succeeding in life? You have haters!
- Somewhere in between? You have haters!

People judge people. People want what others have. People get jealous. People hate. It's a human condition.

There are different types of cynics too. Some are intimidated. You might have friends from high school who follow you on social media. They watch you. They see you succeed, and they get irritated. Some might stop following you, mostly because they are ashamed about some aspect of their life. You intimidate them. That doesn't make them evil or full of hate, but rather they're intimidated and insecure.

Then there are the *real* haters. These are the people to be careful with. They might pretend to be your friends, but really, they are full of hardcore hate. They bleed it. And they bash you publicly with it. That's because these haters are jealous. Your success is their failure.

And don't think that you're not a hater too.

There are people you hate right this moment. Own that nasty part of yourself. Embrace the haters and your own hate. Acknowledge that disliking others and people not liking you is a natural, normal part of being human.

It is the best way to channel the energy in positive, productive ways. Instead of hating and getting nasty, channel the negative emotions into something useful. Use them as motivation to take the action needed to succeed.

Since you have haters no matter what, it's important to learn how to deal with it all.

Here's how:

- **Step 1:** Embrace haters as a part of life.
- **Step 2:** Celebrate. Haters will show you what's great about you and what you need to change. They keep you living big.
- **Step 3:** While they are worried about you growing every day, you just worry about your growth. They chase you while you chase success. Put on a show for them. Let them watch.

Let's talk about how.

EMBRACE THE HATERS

In 2016 and 2017, I started doing Facebook Live events (before it was cool). It felt a little douchey, but it was good for business. "POWERHOME SOLAR here," "Jayson Waller again here," etc. When I put myself out there, I attracted haters.

People would say stuff like, "Dude, that's annoying. Why are you doing that all the time?"

I was doing my job. Staying in my lane. Promoting my business. As the company grew, the haters took note. I would get messages like this from former home security friends in different states: "Hey, man, I'm in California. I'd love to get into solar. Do you ever want to open in California?"

And, lo and behold, many of the alarm company guys I was

friends with back in 2015 were now struggling. Many of them reached out to join my company, get business advice, or go solar themselves. I embraced them.

The simplest way to deal with hate is to get really obsessed with success. When someone hates you, lean into the next action you need to take to get to the next level.

CELEBRATE SUCCESS

Make sure you celebrate your success. Haters will show you what's great and what needs improvement. They keep you successful.

Also get interested in the success of others. Learn from them. Celebrate their wins too.

While I was writing this book, I went to dinner with a dynamic group of friends. One runs several very successful car dealerships. Another is the owner of a $5 million business. The third friend just got out of prison after thirty-two years. His story is being made into a movie. His name is Rick Wershe Jr. You might know him as "White Boy Rick." We are four completely different personalities, with different backgrounds, but we love each other just the same.

That night, we shared our successes and struggles with each other. And we celebrated everybody in the group, what they had achieved, and how far they had come. It was amazing.

Haters worry about your growth every day. They chase you while you chase success. So just worry about your own growth. Get obsessed with success. I love to see people be successful. I love to see them accomplish their goals. I love to help them if I can, and I love to be around people who have more than me. I also love learning from them how I can be better. I always ask, *What can I learn from someone who is doing better than me?*

When someone hates you, turn your focus the other way. Or help them. You know the guys at the trade show who scoffed at me? I have run into a few of them again over the years. Some I've given advice to. Others have approached me for business deals or jobs. What do I do? I bring them into the fold. My favorite tip for turning haters into fans is to love them back and help them.

On Instagram, I can still see my haters watching. Some of them have even become fans. That's made me hungrier to succeed. It drives me harder because I won't let them be right. A $30 million company wasn't enough. Getting to $500 million wasn't either. The more people hate, the more I focus on growing to a $1 billion company. That negativity can be used as fuel to show them what you are really made of.

My fourteen-year-old daughter Londyn is a great example of this tip. She was diagnosed with precocious puberty after she turned nine and had her period. We had to see a specialist to help reverse this process because she was too young. The doctor prescribed a monthly injection, which made her gain a lot of weight. This made her insecure, and she suffered some bullying at school. Liz and I never brought any of it up because she was so tough and did not like to feel less-than. However, in 2018, when she was eleven, we took her off the shot. She decided to start to work on herself, working out and running. None of us are runners in our family, so she was inspiring. She shed over forty pounds and loves her new leaner self. An eleven-year-old got motivated by haters. I love that.

If you're focused on your success, on growing your business, you don't have time to hate anyone in return. As a byproduct of showing them you can, you show them they can too. Make them hungry for their own success.

That's the way to win—through healthy competition and pushing through to the next limit.

HATE IN YOUR LIFE

You can't let haters take control of you. You can't let them beat you down or cause you to question yourself or your own worth.

Hate often happens when people have different perspectives. It can happen when one person feels threatened or intimidated by another person. Jealousy breeds hate. Insecurity breeds hate. Lack of confidence breeds it too.

Here's a great way to drop the hate if it comes up. Start by getting curious about the other person:

- What would make them hate?
- Where did they come from?
- What do they think, believe, and value?
- How did their environment shape them?

If you catch yourself hating, check your ego, and put yourself in the other person's position. The more you understand someone else's behavior and position, the more you release both of you from hate. If you give people or situations a chance without predetermining judgments or outcomes, you'll be amazed what doors will open. Besides, carrying around hate for another person is more destructive to you than it is to them.

You're not doing this for them. You're doing it for you. Holding onto negative thoughts about anyone holds you back.

Remember how Ben and I had a falling out in 2014? Today, he works for POWERHOME SOLAR as our Chief Sales Officer.

Ben wasn't a big hater, but we struggled for a period. To release myself from my own frustrations and repair the relationship, I had to get curious about how he thinks and acts. Once we worked through our differences, we were good. I love the guy. He adds massive value to the company and my life.

Sometimes, hate can be a mirror to a truth you need to see about yourself. Get curious about yourself too. Getting curious is like being a detective. Trying to understand the other person gives you power, while being consumed by hate takes it away. If hate is just feedback, it becomes a tool for growth.

CHANNEL HATER ENERGY WITH A "HATE LIST"

My business partner Kevin and I kept a notepad with a list of names of people who hated us scrawled on it. I'm not kidding. We used it as fuel in the business. We'd read the names when we were frustrated about the growth of our business, and we'd envision the day when these people would want to do business with us. That notepad listed at least twenty people.

The list motivated me. When someone was mean to me to a point where I couldn't get past it, their name went on the list. This turned the negative energy into positive fuel for success. Before I wrote the name down, resentment was controlling me. Once the name was on the list, I got it out. I owned the crap out of those emotions.

When someone hates you and you can't get over it, put their name on your list. Own those negative feelings, and channel them into positive action.

It's important to follow through here—don't read the list to get more resentful and angrier. Use it to purge the bad feelings from your heart. Then, again, focus on your success. As you keep reaching goals and thriving despite their criticism, there are three trajectories the haters may follow:

1. They'll become fans and start loving you.
2. Your success will make them more and more miserable. They'll usually go into a dark abyss at this point—they'll resent you, but they'll go away.
3. They'll stick around, despise you, and follow you on Facebook. They'll let their hate consume them and sometimes get to you. But as the hate grows, it will hold them back more and more. You'll keep on growing.

The idea is to get everyone to choose Door #1. There is no sunshine behind Doors #2 and #3. No free car. No speed boats. No trip for two to Hawaii. Mostly there is just a fuck-you sandwich.

But you can't make anyone do anything they don't want to do. Get successful and hope they'll become a fan, partner, or ally—but don't chase them if they refuse to come around.

Sometimes haters hate because they are suffering. They are stuck. They don't know how to get out of the hole they are in. When they see you succeed, it drives them crazy with rage or envy. But they are hurting. When you've got them on your list, ready for the day that they come around, it's a way to relieve their suffering, if they're open to it. It gives them hope.

With your own negative emotions aside, you can focus on expanding your own thinking. By clearing your mind, you can start to think bigger.

HATERS NEED A BIGGER MISSION

Anyone trying to break someone else down is someone who needs a bigger mission.

Making fun of or judging the way a person looks, how successful they are, or what they do, is hate that comes from insecurity.

A hater might dismiss a person for the way they look or speak. Or because they come from somewhere else. Or because they are undereducated (like me) or overeducated like someone with three or four academic degrees. In some cases, a hater will attack a person's choices, beliefs, or—more commonly these days—political persuasion.

You might not even think you're a hater. But I have news for you. Even if you have a passing thought about someone else that would not be empowering to you or to them if they knew you held that opinion, then you're a hater.

If you've left negative comments on someone's social feed, sorry to say, you're a hater.

People claw other people down when they don't feel good about themselves, which really comes down to not having a big enough mission. So anytime you find yourself hating, look at what you're doing. Expand your mission. It will bring you back to your power.

Racehorses don't look to the horses on their right or left—if they did, they may easily collide at those incredible speeds and become injured or die. So they have blinders on to keep them looking straight ahead! They only see in front of them.

THE BOTTOM LINE ON HATE

By the end of 2015, the business had cash flow problems. It was losing money, and we weren't paying ourselves. In our line of business, the normal practice is to prepay 80 percent of whatever we sell upfront and within sixty days before we see a dollar. So the more we sold, the bigger the cash flow problems became.

Before I hit rock bottom, I reached out to the guy who had bought our former business (as well as dozens of other investors) to try and secure some fast cash to stay afloat.

"Look, I've got $300,000 in accounts—I don't have the cash flow to buy the rest of the equipment because I'm paying for everything upfront," I told them.

No one I called was interested.

"Hey, man, you want to invest in the company? We have all these accounts sold. It's a cash flow problem," I'd say.

"Nah, man, I really don't want to," came some form of the reply, repeatedly.

I went down my list of contacts over the years, and no one would invest. It was 2016, and this was when I sold my lake house and put the money back into the business. Almost $2 million.

Ironically, just after the sale, one of my biggest haters of all time wanted to invest $100,000. I took it, though I didn't need it. We'd used the money from the sale of the lake house, and that helped with the cash flow problems, so all I did with this investment was put in an account as a reserve in case we ever needed it. I never used it, not one penny.

I gave it back three years later. By that time, the money had grown almost eight times, and that investor got a massive payment.

The investor was my mother-in-law.

Remember that we had been on such bad terms that she wouldn't let me see my daughter be born. She hated my guts, talked shit about where I lived, and tried to stop me and my wife from being together because I was "trailer trash." Again, I don't blame—I understand where she was coming from. Still, I had to get over myself to take her money. When I did, it was even more fuel to succeed.

As we listed the lake house for sale, Liz told me that her mom had some money. "Should we ask her for a loan in case we need it?" Liz asked me.

"Fuck no, I don't want a loan from your mom," I said stubbornly.

Liz talked to her mom, and her mom seemed to see it as a worthwhile investment and not a loan. I put the money in a bank account. Then I sold the house and used the payout from it to fund the company and get a bank loan. But I was driven by my mother-in-law's money that sat in that bank account.

When the company bought her out three years later, her investment ended up at eight times what it started at. It felt good. There was no malice or pride. I gave it with grace. Liz's mom and I have come a long way in our relationship. Today, it's one of mutual respect. She wouldn't have invested the money if not, and I couldn't have taken it.

Whenever people say you can't, or you hear a similar negative voice in your head, all you need to do is move forward. Come from a place of, "I can, you can, we all can." Put your head down and take the next step forward.

Your job is to defy the odds.

Everybody has haters, and that's okay. Embrace them. You don't have to like me or love me. Either way, you're watching me. And if you watch me too much, you won't be growing. I'm not watching you. I'm worried about my team, my company, my employees, and my family.

If you see me check in to an exclusive boutique hotel or drive a Lamborghini, be proud of me. Don't judge me. I worked my ass off for it. And if I can, you can.

Nobody sprinkled fairy dust on me or the next guy. Every ounce of energy, every sentence, every hour, every minute spent worrying about someone else will hold you back.

Embrace your haters and focus on success. It's a game-changer.

Here is the other important thing to take note of when building your biggest dreams. Don't be afraid to let go. As an entrepreneur, when you build something from the ground up and know it better than anyone else, it's hard to see inefficiency happen and not want to step in and fix it right away. It's harder when surrounded by haters.

But I learned it's far more important to give people that opportunity and let them either sink or swim. Letting go is so hard, and ignoring the haters is truly what I needed to learn to take our business to the next level. Knowing that would have allowed our business to potentially scale faster than we already have.

CHAPTER CHALLENGE

LOVE YOUR HATERS

Take reflection time to reflect on the haters you know are in your life. Use this section to acknowledge and understand your haters. Go through this series of questions, and better understand how to love your haters. Then rip this page out of the book, and hang it up somewhere you will see it every day—a bathroom mirror, your refrigerator, or the side of your computer monitor. The location doesn't matter, only that you see it every day. To change your underdog story, you must love your haters and act despite the criticism. It becomes easier and easier to do this when you own your power.

1. Who are the biggest critics in your life?

....

....

....

....

....

2. What do they say you cannot achieve that you actually can? **Describe it.**

....

....

....

....

....

3. If you put yourself in their shoes, why do you think they criticize you?

....

....

....

....

....

Once you begin to understand your haters, you can begin to
embrace them, sympathize, and forgive them. For this one, don't
post your lists or thoughts on social media. Keep it private. But do
post that you did the work. Use hashtags #OYPLoveYourHaters,
#OwnYourPower, or #JaysonWaller to acknowledge your haters
and move forward.

CHAPTER SEVEN

PRINCIPLE #7—TEAM OUT

When I was younger, I got results by grinding through what had to be done. No problem was too big. No obstacle was too great. I would just work harder. Just grind through and do whatever it took to get past the problem.

My approach has changed. I still grind and always will, but I also place serious value on relationships. You can work hard by yourself and grind it solo to just get it done. But if you develop great relationships with people you can team up with along the way, you will stoke your own success massively.

It's more than connecting with successful people. You want to take meetings with all types of people from all walks of life.

So many times, I've booked a meeting and felt like skipping it, but I go anyway, and then it changes my life. Being too self-focused gets us in the way of our own success. It stops people from giving, sharing, and asking for help when it's needed.

Relationships exist for us to help and be helped. Coach and be coached. They open doors. They pave new routes you never thought of and provide new ways to make your map. Good relationships will forever change your life.

After moving to Michigan, I met so many good friends and encountered so many eye-opening people. Why? Because I always, always take meetings. I don't discriminate. I'll talk to sales guys, business acquaintances, podcast listeners, billionaires, guys and gals who are starting out, the cashier at Kroger—pretty much anyone who is engaging and willing to connect. And when I do, I am all in.

One meeting comes to mind that I almost didn't take, when someone referred me to an ad agency that shoots TV commercials. Today, they create a lot of our assets, and it led me to doing business with the Detroit Lions.

But it almost didn't happen.

I resisted the meeting because I never wanted to be on TV. I ran a great company. We had a powerful brand, and that was all we needed. It was a chance meeting, set up by a stranger I ran into at the gym. Another relationship that came about by happenstance. His name is Brian Elias, and he is now my friend and business mentor.

Here's how it happened.

I was at the fancy gym that I go to around the corner from my house. I got on one of those stationary bikes—the ones all lit up with a large display and flashing lights. I started the routine, and this guy walked up to me.

"Hey, where'd you get that piece of shit outside?" he said, smirking and pointing out the window.

He had seen me pull into the parking lot in my blue Lamborghini, raise the scissor doors, and step out like some asshole with bleach-blond hair. The Lambo isn't even the best car in the parking lot, but it gets attention.

"I got it from a guy who couldn't afford the gas. Why? You got gas money? Maybe I can take you for a ride?" I threw back at him. He started laughing.

I got back to my biking, but he interrupted me again.

"I noticed it says BAM on your license plate," he chuckled.

"Yeah. It stands for build a movement," I said.

His smile turned into a thoughtful pouted lip, and he nodded. He was impressed. "You're on my bike," he said.

"Well, it looks like you can ride that bike," I said, pointing to another bike in a row of carbon-copy bikes just like the one I was on.

This snarky back-and-forth lasted a few minutes more. It was all in good fun. I could tell he wanted to chat, and I gauged whether I was in the mood. Again, every moment in life we are making decisions. That day I chose to engage him.

He asked me my name and what line of business I was in. I told him. Right away he recognized me as the solar guy. He'd seen some of our mailers and Facebook ads.

Then he introduced himself. "Brian Elias from Hansons Windows and Siding," he said.

Then he sang a jingle: "Your home needs work, call 1-800 Hansons. Get it done." Apparently, I was the only guy in Michigan who didn't know it. Elias had sold his company about eight months earlier for $80 million and had been interested in becoming a board member for another company.

After that, Brian and I hit it off. We had a couple of lunches and became friends. I leaned on him as a CEO coach. He leaned on me for marketing. It worked.

I could have blown him off. I could have shut down the chatter, plugged in my earbuds and ignored him. Instead, I engaged him in conversation.

Eventually, our relationship led to a conversation about an ad agency.

"Hey, you need to meet the Sussman Agency," Brian said. "You guys need to do TV commercials for your business."

Prior to that conversation, we had done some gaudy, horrible commercials. One that I wrote featured the punter and kicker from the Lions, my son, and I doing the floss (a dance move popularized by the video game Fortnite). It also featured a talking dog. Yes, a talking dog. Then we did one with the Cleveland Browns.

That was POWERHOME 1.0. There's no elevator, right? Step one was the shitty commercials.

When I decided to take the meeting with Alan Sussman, I could quickly see he was one of the most genius human beings I'd ever met. He's a seventy-four-year-old Jewish man who rocks sandals and socks all the time.

His partner Dino is an older Italian mafia-type dude who plays golf in long-ass shorts. The pair are characters, and I love them. They're like my family today. But I didn't know that going in.

What kind of dinner am I going to here? Am I wasting my time? Let's see how this goes. It's a meal.

I had one brilliant idea for an emotional commercial, so I decided to pitch it. The scenario was this: a guy comes home. He's tired from work. His wife has a power bill with a graph and a red arrow pointing up. "Honey, I don't think we can afford the power anymore," she says. He says, "Oh," and you hear Morgan Freeman or Sam Elliott or someone cool saying, "Are you tired of high utility rates? Call POWERHOME SOLAR."

I had other ideas. I pushed them too. I thought I was a genius. "What do you think?"

Their excitement didn't match mine.

"How does solar work?" Alan asked.

I went into my usual sermon. The sun hits the panels. The energy then is converted from DC to AC, where you use that energy first. Any extra energy fills up your battery and storage, and you use that at night. Any excess energy above that will go to the meter. The meter runs backward.

You get a credit on your bill. They sell your extra power to your neighbor.

"If your company needed one more sale before you went out of business, who would you want to try to make the sale?" says Alan.

"Shit. Me. I'm the best salesman there is. I can sell solar to anybody."

So that night we decided it made sense to put me in twenty-five million homes. I didn't want to be in TV commercials. But they knew what was best. Like the Jolly Green Giant is the face of canned veggies and the little freckled girl is the face of Wendy's, I had to be the face of POWERHOME SOLAR. Elon Musk is the face of Tesla. Steve Jobs is known for Apple. It made sense. They were right. Though, I did push one last time. "How about we get Morgan Freeman?"

Fast forward: we did an epic commercial with the Detroit Youth Choir at the Fox Theatre. They sang "Let the Sunshine In." I spoke from my heart. Nailed it on the first take. We put my face on all these commercials.

Our sales exploded.

The point of the story isn't my face or my sales ability but how much relationships matter. They are critical for success in life. When you open yourself up to other people, they push you, help you grow, and help you win.

If you want to live your best life or be successful at anything, you must team out.

SMALL INTERACTIONS NOW LEAD TO BIG OUTCOMES LATER

When it comes to relationships, sometimes you have an interaction one day that leads to a connection later. Eventually it can all lead to a major win. I've experienced it several times.

Back when I did home security, a guy named Allen wanted to sit down. He bugged me for a long time. I thought meeting with him would be a waste of time. So I blew him off. But Allen was one persistent guy. Finally, when another meeting I was supposed to have got canceled, I took his call. Allen convinced me that day to partner with him.

Our work together added 50 percent more profit to my business over the next two years.

You don't know what's going to happen when you meet people. You don't know the difference they're going to make in your life. And it's not just high-powered people. It's all people. My bad judgments about Allen got in the way of a smart partnership for two years.

One small exchange can lead to another one, which can lead to another one. Every decision we make every single day changes our lives forever.

The relationship with the Detroit Lions ultimately led to my friendship with Barry Sanders. (More on that in the next chapter.)

When I moved to North Carolina, my dad asked me which high school I wanted to go to, Concord or Gastonia. I chose Concord. Had I not gone to that school, I wouldn't have met my wife at Central Cabarrus High School. We wouldn't have built an incredible life together or have our kids and our grandkids.

My buddy Joe, who is one of my best friends, chose to move from New York to work for me. If he hadn't, he wouldn't have met his wife, Ashley. They have five kids. We met playing video games in 2003.

All our lives intersect. It's easy to put off meetings or social interactions some days. But choosing to connect with people is one of the most important decisions you can make. Embrace connection and capitalize on relationship-building opportunities with all types of people, especially on the days you don't want to.

EVERYONE IS AN ASSET

When people are negative, it's healthy to tune them out and focus more on you. But with everyone else, you must take the blinders off.

I've been poor. I've been mocked. I've been made fun of. I've been told I can't. I've had money. I've been successful. I've been celebrated. It feels like I've been on both ends of the spectrum of life and most points in between.

Here's what I've learned: all people have value.

The people I am friends with are all very different. In 2018, my wife and I planned a couples' trip with our friends. We went to Turks and Caicos with a mixed bag of friends, twenty-two people altogether.

On one of the outings, some of us went out on a boat together. We had Detroit Lions kicker Matt Prater and his wife with us, my buddy who is a tax accountant and his wife, and a wealth management friend and his wife. We all have different incomes, lifestyles, and nationalities, but we're all friends.

Once a month, we all come together to play games, and we always look to invite more couples. Our group grows bigger all the time as new people come into our circle. I love when friends meet friends.

We have a tradition on birthdays where everyone takes turns speaking around the table. Each person tells the birthday boy or girl what they appreciate about them, or they share a funny story about them. My friends did this for me when we went to Turks on my birthday. I even got emotional, which almost never happens.

That night, I basked in how awesome it was to have these very different people in my life. Some of them make $50,000 per year. Some of them make $500 million. It doesn't fucking matter. We're all more successful because we have each other.

When you go to meetings to build relationships, be open and optimistic about everyone. Mix it up. Be open-minded. You never know who will teach you the lesson you need to learn, connect you with a person you need to meet, or give you an opportunity that boosts your mission. For the networking businessperson, possibilities are everyone.

People want to be a part of your life. People need you to be a part of their life. Networking with other people helps everyone achieve greater outcomes faster. And life is way more fun too.

DO YOU SEE PEOPLE?

Relationships take work. We're all guilty of not putting in effort sometimes. We move too fast. We get caught up in our agendas and the details of life. We forget to really see people. We spend time with them, but sometimes we aren't there with them. I'm guilty of this too.

In the end, people just want to feel valued. No matter how much money they make. No matter what their background is. No matter where they live. We all are desperate to be seen.

So when you are with another person and you are fully there, it's a damn gift. Be all in when you're with family, friends, colleagues, acquaintances, and strangers, even. I've found you get more than one gift back. It's more like a truckload.

CHAPTER CHALLENGE

TEAM OUT

Take reflection time to reflect on the quality of your relationships. Use this section to acknowledge and understand your network and how the people in your life can be additive to achieving your goals. Go through this series of questions, and better understand how you can build your network and expand your contacts in business. Then rip this page out of the book, and hang it up somewhere you will see it every day—a bathroom mirror, your refrigerator, or the side of your computer monitor. The location doesn't matter, only that you see it every day. To change your underdog story, you must network, build a tribe, and team up with like-minded individuals. A vibrant and growing network of people will help you own your power.

1. Who in your current network can add value to your business?

....

....

....

....

....

2. Are there people on social media who can be a part of your virtual support team when it comes to business?

....

....

....

....

....

3. Are you willing to put the time and energy into keeping a team together? **Circle One.**

Yes / No

Once you begin to understand how to team up and use a combined set of resources together, success starts to feel easier. Celebrate a person in your life both privately and on social media. Post about it if you want to share with the Own Your Power community. Use hashtags #OYPTeamOut, #OwnYourPower, or #JaysonWaller to celebrate your wins.

CHAPTER EIGHT

PRINCIPLE #8—FOCUS ON THE PLAY-BY-PLAY

My dad and I didn't have the best relationship when I was younger. He was tough on me as a kid. But my fondest memories of time with my dad centered around our favorite football team, the Detroit Lions.

My dad is from Michigan. My mom is from North Carolina. The only sports I was ever allowed to watch were teams from Detroit, though I grew up in Arizona and North Carolina.

We watched the "Bad Boys" (Detroit Pistons) in basketball and the Red Wings in hockey (who were horrible at the time and didn't gain any traction until the '90s). And so, of course, for football it was the Lions, who sucked until '89. That is when Barry Sanders was drafted.

Every Sunday, my pops and I would go to the bar around the

corner from our house to watch the Lions play. These were the days of the satellite dish. We couldn't afford to bolt one onto the roof of our home in Arizona. And forget the subscription fee for the football package too. There was just no money for that.

So my dad and I would meet his buddy, another Lions fanatic, at a crappy little pub with an aging bar lined with swivel bar stools, which were a highlight for a kid. They knocked back beers, and I drank my soda as we watched the Lions play. The bar also laid out salty peanuts in their shells in community bowls. We cracked them, ate the nuts, and threw the shells on the floor.

I became a hardcore Sanders fan from the moment I watched his first game against the Arizona/Phoenix Cardinals in '89, when he ran for about seventy-one yards.

"Here he goes! Whoa, look at him go. He's still going!" we screamed at the screen.

Watching the Lions was a tradition even after we moved to North Carolina. Eventually, we did get a satellite dish on the side of our trailer, complete with a DirectTV package so we could watch the games every Sunday. Some years later, after saving hard, we drove up to Michigan around Thanksgiving to watch the games in person at the stadium.

Since Barry Sanders joined the team in 1989, I have either watched every Lions game on TV or attended the games in person. I have skipped funerals. I have missed birthday parties. I have rear-ranged picnics and holiday gatherings to make sure I see every single Lions game. I even have a Lions tattoo. I'm not kidding.

You know those assholes who paint themselves up at games and yell and scream and act like idiots? That's me and my friends. A clip of us was used in a commercial that ran for years, with our faces all painted up in blue. ESPN posted a video of us on its website back in 2010. And in the back of my mind, I always thought it would be cool to meet Barry.

After building three successful businesses and grinding through twenty-five different jobs, sweating it out on my roller coaster of a life, I reached a pivotal point. In 2018, just before I turned thirty-nine, POWERHOME SOLAR signed a deal to install solar for the Detroit Lions.

The day Kevin and I signed the deal, we called my dad. It was Kevin's idea, so he dialed my dad's number, and we put him on speaker. "We're putting solar on Ford Field," Kevin said.

"No shit?" my dad said.

My pops is a very quiet man. He's reserved. He doesn't say a lot. And he doesn't get emotional. But I knew he was proud that day. We were finally making it big.

Remember, each moment adds to the next. Each step leads to where you want to go. I was taking the stairs. I had big aspirations for the company, but I was always focused on the play-by-play.

SMALL STEPS TO BIG DREAMS

As is tradition in my family, my son has become a huge Lions fan and a fan of the punter Sam Martin in particular, who now plays for the Broncos. After the solar deal with the Detroit Lions, I also cut a deal with Sam to shoot a commercial with us on Ford Field.

Imagine this: I am in the stadium that is home to my favorite football team, putting my business product on their roof, and filming a commercial on the field with one of the players both my son and I love. Sam also brought in Matt Prater, the Lions kicker, so we could meet him too. Both players have since become close friends of ours.

After shooting the commercial that day, POWERHOME SOLAR continued to grow, and I eventually moved the family to Michigan. In 2018, I sat with Kevin in my office, spitballing some ideas.

"What if we could get Barry Sanders in one of our commercials?"

It was a blue-sky idea. A someday brain fart that we enjoyed dreaming up. We had done commercials with the Lions, the Browns, and the Panthers. I met a few players here and there, and I had become friends with Matt and Sam. I met a few more of the Lions players too. And because of all the work POWER-HOME SOLAR was doing, we made an impact in the community of Detroit, Michigan.

So one night I was invited to Rod Wood's home. Today he is the Lions' president. Back then he was the vice president for the team. I was a season ticket holder and a sponsor. And Barry Sanders was there.

I was chatting with a group of other party people when I saw Barry out of the corner of my eye. Some advice: you can't act like a fan when you see someone famous because that's what everybody does. You must be different. So I walked around the party with some swagger and confidence, like everyone should be a fan of me. I was not arrogant and cocky, and you shouldn't be either. You want to be warm, but also kind of intriguing and mysterious.

> **Big dreams are important. But if you get too caught up in the future, you can easily get off track. It can become overwhelming. Focus on the play-by-play. Goal-set no more than six months out. Achieve small milestones toward the goal. Then one day you'll be there, living your dream life, and it's better than you ever imagined.**

While fanboys might ask for a selfie, I avoid that lame behavior. I walked up and introduced myself: "Jayson Waller, POWER-HOME SOLAR." I had no agenda. I didn't want his picture or autograph. I was glad Barry was there. It was great to meet him. But it wasn't a big deal, right?

Barry and I had a nice exchange that night. I told him a story about how I almost died in a plane once. It sounds horrible, but it's funny when I act it out. After that night, his agent called me, and he became an influencer for our brand. In the process, we became good friends.

At Christmas, I invited him to our holiday party. My dad came too. That night, I sat across from them both, and I watched my pops eat dinner with Barry. My dad is perhaps one of the biggest Barry Sanders fans of all time (second only to me!). This was a "wow" moment for me. And we were still just taking the stairs.

Soon after that, Barry and I did a commercial together. The morning of the shoot, it hit me how cool it was to be doing this blue-sky project. As I sat at the edge of the bed thinking about the day ahead, Liz smiled at me and said, "You know you're getting ready to do a commercial with your favorite player of all time, right?"

I tried to play it cool with Liz, though she knows me better than that. When I got in the shower, it hit me. Holy shit! After all this hard work, grinding it for a couple of decades, with all the highs and lows, all the frickin' haters, I was doing a commercial with Barry.

I drove a Ferrari to the commercial shoot that day. Barry and I crushed it in front of the camera. It was epic. I've watched him play since I was ten. He is an icon and my football hero. Today, Barry and I are friends. Our kids talk and hang out. He has been on my podcast. And I give him business advice.

Then there's Matt Prater, who is now one of my closest friends too. All the little actions added up in a wild way where I achieved a dream so cool that I never thought it was possible, not even five years ago.

It amazes me what dreams can be achieved when you focus on the play-by-play.

I didn't set out in business thinking, *One day I'll be a billionaire, and I will become friends with Barry Sanders and other NFLers, and we'll eat burgers at my place and spend my birthday in Turks.* It wasn't imaginable for me.

I had small goals. I wanted to open an office. I want to grow it and add sales reps, a few at a time. I kept setting those kinds of small goals. If you stay in the moment, focus on small wins, you will continue to get closer to your big dream goals.

Too many people put way too much pressure on themselves by aiming way too high. Then it freaks them out and becomes unattainable. Massive goals are great for motivation, but you've gotta chunk it down. Stay the course and focus on small milestones. Incremental progress is the way. Who's your Barry? Maybe one day you'll sit with them. Just make sure you're taking the stairs to get there.

GET YOUR HEAD OUT OF THE CLOUDS

Too many people get overly focused on their massive dreams and then stop themselves from living the dream life they desperately want. They psych themselves out.

They start believing there is too much disparity between where they are and where they want to get to. They tell themselves it's not possible, or they start thinking it's too big and that they should get more practical. Some people realize where they want to go is too far from where they are now, and they feel like crap. They relate to dreams as ideas that are mostly unattainable.

It's hard to get inspired and get into action if you've psyched yourself out.

If you don't consider how to get to those big dreams, which can include owning your highly successful company, if you can't see the next steps to take, the dream may stay in your head forever. It becomes a "someday" goal, and then that someday may never come. Too many people die with dreams in their heads because they don't get practical about the actions they need to take to get there.

That means you need to set two kinds of goals: big dream goals and small winnable goals.

When you need to feel inspired and motivated, think about the big dream goal. When you need to focus on the next action to move you toward that dream, focus on the little targets you need to hit in the next day, week, or month.

POWERHOME SOLAR has developed partnerships with five professional football franchises (Carolina Panthers, Cleveland Browns, Detroit Lions, Indianapolis Colts and Pittsburgh Steelers), one professional baseball franchise (Cleveland Indians/Guardians), and one university (NC State) to help reduce grid energy consumption and promote the use of solar energy.

Right now, if I say that POWERHOME SOLAR is going to go public and be worth $50 billion, that's a dream goal. We probably will go public soon. It's exciting. But to get there, I need to focus on the moment.

Next year we might be a $2 billion company, but only if I focus on the next three months and then the next three after that. This chunking strategy helps me stay in the moment, stay inspired, and stay in action.

Set goals today, this week, this month. Set them even for the next three months or the next six months, but stop there. Stay focused using small blocks of time. When you focus on small winnable goals on the way to a big one, you maintain control.

Small goals have a domino effect. A bunch of those wins will achieve your big dream objective. And then when you accomplish that, you can set a new dream goal and find the winnable goals along the way. Keep moving the blocks and letting the dominoes fall, and the dream will eventually be realized.

If you get frustrated, feel defeated, or get pissed about your progress, think about the big dream goal again. It will help you stay focused and grounded. Any time you have an idea where you think, *Holy shit, that's next level,* use that potent dream to get inspired.

If you only think about your situation now, you aren't aiming for anything. You're not making your map because you have no destination to navigate toward. But at the same time, if all you have is a destination that's far away, your drive isn't going to be fun. You might feel hopeless about ever getting there too. Oscillating between the two types of goals is the key to staying grounded, motivated, and in action.

REVERSE ENGINEERING

The best way to break down the work that it takes to achieve a big dream is to reverse engineer it. Think of what you want. Get excited about it, and then consider where you are today. In three months (and no more than six months), where would you like to be?

Let's say you want to lose fifty pounds. You might think about what you'll look like, what you'll do, how you'll feel. A big dream should fire you up.

But then you must think about where you are at. You aren't going to lose all that weight in one day, one week, or one month even. It's not healthy. So you break those fifty pounds down into small goals so it is more attainable. The first goal is two pounds. It's the same for the following week. By the end of the month, you'll have lost eight pounds. That's exciting!

It's not complicated, but you do have to remind yourself to stay in your "now block." You must push away any noise in your head or negative self-talk and just look at the next three months.

Focus on the small targets that are easy to achieve, and you'll build confidence and momentum as you achieve each small goal. Maybe you start with a trainer who designs one type of weight routine, and once you lose twenty pounds, you reassess. By focusing on small targets, you can adapt your strategy as you go to achieve results faster.

We live in a digitally connected world that has trained us to seek immediate gratification more than ever. Anyone who wants to watch another episode of their favorite binge-worthy show on Netflix can do that. If I need to find out what the hell the acronym EBITDA means, I can Google it for a fast answer. When my business partner needs to get me a message, he just sends a text. No more answering machines. Instant information. Instant gratification.

Small win goals help you feed your need for immediate gratification, and that keeps you motivated and on track.

My son Christian wants to be an NFL player. I encourage him to play big, and he does.

"Dude, I love that you have that goal and that dream," I said to him. But I've also told him to keep it real or it won't happen. So we break it down. Focus on starting right now in fourth grade.

Then focus on getting on the travel team next summer. Then we focus on how he is doing in middle school. If we stay in the moment and continue to focus on incremental progress—and he still wants this dream—the small wins will build his confidence and skill. All the momentum could lead to going pro.

If he focuses too much on going pro, he could easily psych himself out or miss what he needs to do. He could forget to enjoy the process. The small wins get us there—as long as we have a big dream we're building toward.

WHAT'S YOUR BAM?

The night I accepted the 2019 Ernst & Young Emerging Entrepreneur of the Year Award, I stood on a stage looking out at a crowd of designer tuxedos and gowns. I ended my speech with this:

"At POWERHOME SOLAR, we have an acronym. It's BAM. It stands for building a movement. And so we say we're building a movement one home, one solar panel, one employee at a time. Join me. Say it with me," I told the room of MBAs.

Then the entire room erupted with: "BAM."

I trademarked the BAM acronym long before that night. BAM is on the license plate of my car. It's now on shirts and hats that we use as giveaways for podcast listeners. I live by BAM. You should too.

Here's what BAM is about.

It is a saying that informs a way of life and describes a quality to embrace. It helps people dream big and act big. It's also a mindset and way to be. And anyone can use BAM to figure out what their big dream goals are.

It came about because a former business partner of mine used to say "boom" so much that it became a joke. People who knew him imitated him with love. We would say boom this, boom that. "I'm going to grab a coffee. Boom!"

One day, I was playing the Avengers video game with my son. I kept hitting his character. Every time I did, I said, "Boom!" But the players were making a bam sound when they hit each other, so my son corrected me.

"Dad, stop saying boom. It's bam. Bam is cooler," he said, schooling me.

From that day forward, I used BAM to express when I was fired up. It could be for anything. The company decided not to use Chinese-made solar; we were sticking to American. BAM! The family was on vacation, and we were sitting on a beach. BAM! I got a slick haircut. BAM!

So I started thinking about how to use BAM as an acronym in my business. Then I came up with build a movement, which resonated so deeply with me and the way I want to live my life that I trademarked it.

But really, BAM can stand for anything you want it to. And it doesn't only help people think about what they want to achieve but also how they achieve their goals. BAM is a feeling. It's a way to behave.

It's a quality that captures a spirit of living bold and big and leading the way. Say BAM, and right away you feel good. Try it. BAM! You feel more confident now, don't you?

The BAM mindset can be activated at any time. Now that I interview the most successful people in the world on my podcast, most of them are BAMers without knowing it. They live for causes greater than themselves. They take bold actions. BAM!

BAM will help set your big dream goals. Remember when we talked about living for a cause greater than yourself? What's your BAM? Do you know?

The great thing about POWERHOME SOLAR is that our motto is Building a Movement, or BAM for short. We do that one solar panel, one customer, and one employee at a time. We are building a movement of clean, green energy, and that not only helps customers potentially save money but also does a great thing for the planet. It's easy for our employees to understand and get behind our mission because of the amount of good we can do for customers. I am very blessed to have a chance to lead this company.

Set your big dream goal today. Then reverse engineer it. Be in this moment now. Be in the next moment when that happens. And you'll get there. You'll see. One day you'll be clinking a glass with your version of Barry Sanders and making a difference. You'll have the business of your dreams. That's the way to think. BAM is what life's about.

CHAPTER CHALLENGE

FOCUS ON THE PLAY-BY-PLAY

Take reflection time to consider the big, important things in life. Use this section to reverse engineer your goals and the path to achieve them. Go through this series of questions, and better understand how you can build milestones in business. Then rip this page out of the book, and hang it up somewhere you will see it every day—a bathroom mirror, your refrigerator, or the side of your computer monitor. The location doesn't matter, only that you see it every day. To change your underdog story, you need to look at the life you're building as a movement. It's time to own your power.

1. If your life were dedicated to one movement where you shaped the world in a positive way, what would it be? **Describe it.**

....

....

....

....

2. What are your next steps? What are your first action items?

....

....

....

3. What are experiences you don't want anyone else to go
    through that you know about and know solutions for?

....

....

....

Consider where you are today and where you want to be over
the next three months. Stick to three-month increments of time.
What is one three-month milestone that gets you closer to your
goal? Plot the action items you need to get there. Declare your
BAM or share your three-month milestone. Post about either of
these items if you want to share with the Own Your Power community. Use hashtags #OYPBeAWorldChamp, #OwnYourPower,
or #JaysonWaller.

CONCLUSION

At one point, this chapter was going to be called You're Fucked if You Only Chase Money; Focus on Fulfillment Instead. I still like the title. It sums up this discussion well. If we all lived by that principle, we'd get where we wanted to get. But instead, I thought it should be my concluding message to you.

It's not complicated, but it is important. And remember, this is coming from a guy who people think has "made it." Trailer park to billionaire, right? Underdog to alpha. I drive a Lambo; I must have it all.

Let me tell you the truth about success. It's quite simple.

Fulfillment = Success

A lot of people chase money. They want to open a business to get rich. "I'm going to start my business and drive a Tesla, Cadillac, Porsche, or Hummer," they say.

That is nice, but if that's what you're chasing, you're going after the wrong thing. What you want is to be fulfilled. That's what you need to chase. Any time you take an action, produce a result, and feel a deep sense of joy from the achievement, that's a signal to do more of that. It will help you know that you are on the right path.

Money won't fulfill you. It's nice. It makes life prettier and easier at times. But it doesn't fill you up. Pursue fulfillment instead. Usually, financial security is part of that, though there are plenty of people who don't have much money at all and are fulfilled. They're happy with what they do.

They're comfortable in their skin. They don't owe anybody anything. They go to work every day, or they own their business, or whatever it is they do. They feel great when they go to bed. They feel accomplished.

You can't buy that. I don't care how much money you make. You can't buy fulfillment. You must chase what's inside.

What brings you joy? What fills you up? It evolves as your map changes in life, so ask yourself regularly.

For me, I want to empower other people to be successful. I want other people to achieve things they didn't think they could. A lot of that is running a business. I do that by mentoring sales guys and colleagues. I do it by sharing my entrepreneurial strategies with other businesspeople. I do that by talking to people on my podcast and broadcasting our conversations. I do it by writing this book.

And when I'm doing that, I hear all these great stories. People who didn't have a pot to piss in are now buying their first house for their family to live in. That's the best feeling in the world: to know that you had an impact—that you gave them an opportunity to do that. You know that they're more likely to pay it forward, to help the next guy or gal succeed.

I'm not going to say I don't like to have nice things. Of course I like nice stuff, and I never had nice things as a kid. Now that I do, I like it. I've got a nice watch, nice shoes, nice car, nice house. Great family.

It sure beats the bus and a trailer and peanut butter sandwiches at a motel on a budget trip to Disneyland. But things are just things. They depreciate. You get to decide what you really want and how you're going to get there.

This book you're reading is just a book. It's just nice to have, or it's loaded with insights. You can put it on the shelf or use it as a playbook to get what you want. You get to decide.

I say go make your map. Use what you've learned. Come back to it as often as you need to. Put the principles in action. Change your life. BAM! I know you will.

You're no underdog when you own your adversity and use it to win.

By now you know that's just a myth you made up to stay stuck. Time to bury it. No excuses. Get moving. Your next steps are right in front of you.

BAM!

Own your power!

ACKNOWLEDGMENTS

I would like to acknowledge the following people who have inspired, coached, and pushed me to be all I can be:

- Liz and my four kids.
- My mom Sherry and my dad Bill Waller.
- My siblings Jessi Gandy and Jeremy Waller.
- My best friend and business partner Kevin Klink.
- My brother-in-law Kenny Klinger.
- My business executive team and partners Ben Brookhart, Steve Murphy, Juan Ramirez, and Zack Darrow.
- My coaches David Meltzer, Steve Olsher, and Brian Elias.
- My friend and mentor Alan Sussman.
- My mentor Vince Feranda.
- My book coach Heather Monahan, who pushed and coached me to write a book.
- My Scribe Kay Walker.
- My friends and associates who I featured in this book, including Brian Wolfe, Joe Caban, Dino Rotondo, Matt Prater, John

Leblanc, Rick Wershe Jr, Jeff Fratarcangeli, David Nurse, JT McCormick, Barry Sanders, and others.
- I want to thank all the employees of POWERHOME SOLAR. We are truly building a movement.
- I want to thank many of you on the *True Underdog* podcast and the YAP team that supports the podcast.
- Hala Taha, thank you for your friendship as well.

I also want to acknowledge all the haters out there who put me down and said I'd never make it. Without you, none of this would have been possible.

There are so many more, but I cannot list them all.

Thank you, everyone.

CPSIA information can be obtained
at www.ICGtesting.com
Printed in the USA
BVHW031351270122
627058BV00002BA/2/J